UNBUILT

UNBUILT

Christopher Beanland

BATSFORD

CONTENTS

PREVIOUS PAGE The North-South Axis of Welthauptstadt Germania (see pages 34–41).

RIGHT Rolling pavements: a vision for post-war Berlin (see pages 44–49).

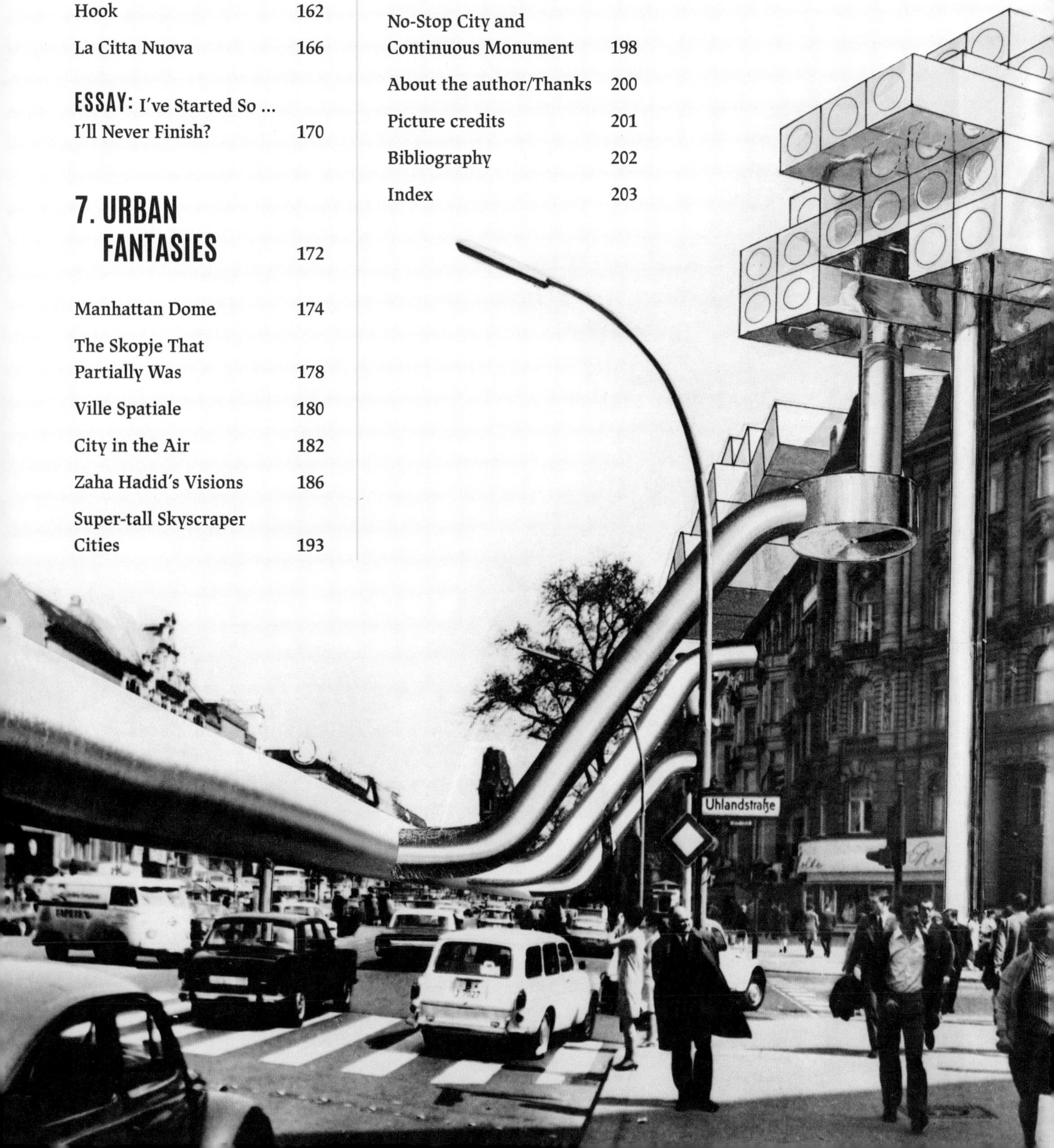
Uhlandstraße

INTRODUCTION

Every human life is a series of failures. Every night we dream, every morning we plan. Everything is seemingly up for grabs. Everything we want, everything we crave. A whole world of everythings. 'Everything means nothing to me,' sang Elliott Smith. One day we go up in smoke or down into the ground, having achieved a fraction of the things we set out to – the ambitious and the creative will have done slightly more than the average.

An architect or a planner's life is this model but supercharged – many will never see a single design downloaded from brain to earth and remade in three dimensions, most will manage a few, some will give up altogether. It's very rare to be able to build a lot, rarer still for what you make to be what you want to make. Buy an architect a drink and listen to the reality, their reality: half of them draw up crap for money and are as disillusioned as a duck stuck in a car park. Most of what's on the books is the meat-and-potatoes stuff no book will ever discuss: the endless faceless flats, the big-box retail, the budget hotels.

The few lives we celebrate are akin to the few buildings and plans we celebrate – the rest is a mediocre mess, just a lot of stuff in the middle. 'Every life is both ordinary and extraordinary,' mulls Logan Mountstuart in William Boyd's *Any Human Heart*, a novel that distils the elemental essence of what life actually means. Mountstuart keeps dreaming, keeps trying; a lesson for us. Each loss, each failure, is just a necessary part of life. 'A horrible thought: could this be the pattern of my life ahead? Every ambition thwarted, every dream stillborn?' To be in a position of being able to dream, to try, to express one's creativity, is a privilege, particularly a Western middle-class privilege – though not a privilege that's particularly well paid until one clambers to the top of the greasy pole – brickies legendarily out-earn junior architects. Everyone out-earns writers. What do we want from a society? Evidently people good with their hands, celebrities, estate agents and yet more hedge-fund managers.

'A little less conversation, a little more action,' sang Elvis. It could be the architect's theme song. For so much is a discussion, a proposal, an attempt. Even when the t's have been crossed and the i's have been dotted and the foundations have been sunk it's no guarantee that the project will be finished. Look at the things that never got completed, like Watkin's Tower in Wembley or the Palace of the Soviets in Moscow.

Most ideas don't get this far. Maybe 90 per cent of what architects do is some level of theorizing; 10 per cent involves donning a hard hat. The hard hat is so seldom worn that the on-site brigade can easily spot how uneasily the yellow plastic crown sits atop the pate. That's the architect – we could just look for the one person wearing all black instead (good luck trying that ruse in Berlin though).

Architecture is an ideas business, a words and drawings business, a thought business even. The attempt is to improve. To improve one has to innovate. Innovation doesn't sit well though, least of all in Britain where the Second Industrial Revolution petered out decades ago, where an entire manufacturing industry is put in museums and where the modernist behemoths of the 1950s to the 1970s have mostly been knocked down. On Sunday afternoons we drive the car to famous buildings from well before that fecund period and admire them, then we drink tea and eat scones and reflect on what we've seen while we read recipes and interviews and blind-date aftermaths in the supplements. Maybe we should be visiting the archives instead and looking at infamous sketches of buildings and admiring them and wondering why they exist on paper rather than on the skyline. We fetishize what's been done, we worry about what's yet to be done and we ignore what's not done. Innovation comes from the latter two.

Turning theory into built reality is a fag, yet it's not as complex as Robert Hughes's assumption about art: that the artist turns feeling into meaning. That is alchemy. Architecture is craft

– far from easy, but with a set of rules to follow, parameters, guides, regulations and a huge amount of (as with films and publishing – thanks, editors!) unrecognized teamwork alongside the auteur. Anyone who labours under the misapprehension that that one 'starchitect' designed that new museum you enjoyed fleetingly is barking up the wrong tree, just as the idea that I am the sole person involved in getting this book into your hands is meretricious. An artist has a patron but doesn't have to take as much shit from them as an architect has to take from a client. But then an artist is a genius (well ...) and an architect a realist (well, mostly). When we talk about failed architecture, how often is it the client who has lost faith, cut corners, slashed budgets, failed to get 'buy-in' from 'stakeholders' to get things moving? Other forces can prevent the reality happening too: community action – which grew exponentially throughout the twentieth century, like environmental protest, locals saying no. It's a valid point: no one wants things done to them. If a road is going to be ploughed through your park, or your favourite community centre is going to be bulldozed, you've every right to be pissed off about it. Add in planning controls, changes of political regime, changes of priorities, money running out, war breaking out, architects burning out, um ... pandemics.

Architecture happens at a grandmotherly pace: it's no wonder things slip through the cracks when the project you're designing today may not top out for 10 years; much can change in the intervening period. It's a wonder anything gets done.

If we're discussing the unbuilt, we also need to remind ourselves that just because a building is built, its story isn't over. When is a building finished? It is no more settled than we could say a human is finished when it arrives. Throughout the life of human or building many changes will happen – improvements, ill-thought-out renovations, degradations.

Architecture has sought to improve the world (mostly – ignore today's rampant neo-liberal need for development dosh for a second). Theoreticians wanted something better. They've not always been listened to. Throughout history, from the first time we lined stones up, plans have been concocted – and although in this book we concentrate on the twentieth century, because the richest ideas of all come from that era, there are also instructive lessons from before the 1900s. Antonio di Pietro Averlino, or Filarete to his mates down the pub in Florence, was always on about his idealized city of Sforzinda in the 1450s. Moving beyond mere architecture, beyond one building towards building many, we see a long lineage of supersized visions that challenged the very way life was conducted. People have consistently sought to change the way other people behave. That process speeded up (as did every other facet of life) in the twentieth century. Example: the three-dimensional city idea that permeated like salad cream through Mothers Pride bread in the post-war world. The idea of putting pedestrians up above cars became a secular religion. The pedestrians in question never fully bought in to these doctrinal decrees, as the desire lines and vaulted barriers and windswept walkways attested to.

'Place the city centre where maximum civic drama might be achieved.'

KENNETH BROWN, INTRODUCTION TO HUBERT DE CRONIN HASTINGS'S *CIVILIA*, 1971

An alternative title for this book could have been 'Maximum Civic Drama'. When the visions were so extraordinary and the world had reached the high point of social democracy, cheap energy and ambition during that golden age of the twentieth century – a state never to be returned to? – we saw expressions of unbridled creativity and flights of fancy.

After the Second World War the dreams were bigger than they had been at any time in history. And much was built with gusto and optimism and sometimes ignored humanism – as John Grindrod's *Concretopia* outlines particularly well. Modernism unleashed a brave new world. There was, in Berlin, Tokyo and Coventry (among the many other cities ruined by the idiocy and violence that Ballard rightly pointed out was our defining human characteristic) tabula rasa which made *grand projets* possible; desirable even. These visions were sold as attainable utopias. OK, an idea is one thing, but words (how I wish this wasn't necessarily so) alone don't always pique sufficient interest. How else do you characterize what's not there? In the era before the internet, World's Fairs and Expos showed punters – who lapped it all up – what living in the future would be like. The national and corporate stands proffered dioramas, moving walkways, public art and Disney-engineered rides that showcased new worlds of automated cars, of multiple levels, of space travel and high-tech homes filled with gadgets. Films like the Eames's explanation of how Saarinen's Washington Dulles Airport would work with its mobile lounges ferrying lazy passengers to their planes or the many motor-industry movies like General Motors' 'Motorama' showing automated cars expanded on what was, apparently, to come. Progress was everything, at all costs. It was accepted.

Dreamy visions of the future that would arrive (but didn't) have become retro-futurist nostalgia – look at the video for Alvvays' single 'Dreams Tonite', spliced together from snapshots of Montreal's Expo '67. We've never been more interested in past visions of the future and less interested in our future. Perhaps we're terrified about what our future will bring. Sixty years ago we were being ushered into a future that brimmed – so the soothsayers said – with abundance and leisure (just forget about the nuclear bombs and you'll be fine). Hundreds of record sleeves feature brutalist architecture on their covers (and Montreal's Bucky dome; see locals Arcade Fire). Back in the twentieth century these visions were potent. Architects and planners had to sell their ideas, and many of those ideas sank. But even if they did, what we're left with has a certain power – like Dieter Urbach's collages of Berlin ladies basking beneath bloated blocks of Plattenbau. Sarah Hardacre's modern-day mixing of modernist 'eyesores' with 1960s pin-ups makes you wonder what we're more offended by now: high rise concrete utopias or bare breasts?

At Montreal's Expo and Osaka's in 1970 the dreams were the biggest of all. Architects and planners were at the high point of modernism, but they were also dancing on the deck of the *Titanic*. Their last big blowouts were the space-age propositions like the No-Stop City, which went on indefinitely. Megastructure projects had gone crazy in the 60s, buildings were getting bigger, cities were getting wilder. A cursory glance at any issue of *Concrete Quarterly* from 1964 to 1974

'A wrong-headed hierarchy of realities grants primacy to a breezeblock over a painting of a breezeblock.'

JONATHAN MEADES

shows an almost unending series of ever more bulbous (which would be soon seen as bilious, sadly) projects, mouth-watering and eye-opening and utterly compelling. An interesting sidenote though: CQ regularly championed 'streetscape' and schemes that seemed to blend in with the environment, despite those very same projects being perceived retrospectively as being 'too much'. They weren't designed to be inhuman, on the contrary – that epithet was applied later, and not by everyone. The greatest period of building in human history, an epoch condensed to a decade, a brutalist blowout. Why not have a crack? If everyone else was building exciting things why not try too?

Sometimes you look at what was not built and you think it must have been a slender call – the girl that almost went on that date with you, the shot that hit the post, the exam you almost got a first in, the referendum that nearly went the right way – life's 'yeses' and 'nos' are tighter than you could ever believe. Why do some things happen and some things not happen? We look for patterns, for certainty, for reason. The truth is that sometimes there is none. The belief is no longer in God or grand narratives (both can be pernicious; one has the possibility at least of making things better). Sometimes error, bad luck, a missed train, a bad mood, a storm, can change the course of the story. You can plan as much as you like (and hell knows architects and planners like to) but sometimes things just don't work out. Why? Because life doesn't always fall into place. Chance is much underplayed in philosophy. The flâneur recognizes randomness as essential, existential even. Architecture seeks to impose rationality on to chaos. Its end results sometimes create chaos where once there was simplicity. And with its journey being so meandering and messy it mirrors life. Guido, the exasperated film director in Fellini's bravura *8½*, could equally be an architect, just as the title of the movie could equally have been the original *La Bella Confusione* ('The Beautiful Confusion') because life resists attempts to shape it and sometimes one must embrace that and see the beauty in everything that can't be controlled.

But we wanted to organize, to rationalize. We want to as humans. That urge has perhaps diminished today. It's not entirely gone, there'll always be a part of us like that – but we are more cautious. In the post Covid-19 epoch we are all scared little children, our sensitivity to risk shot. Everyone is paranoid – especially about each other. Planners were in the ascendancy in the twentieth century though, experts were, their expertise was. Patrick Abercrombie's many and wholesale visions of London and especially its road network were radical. Like Abercrombie, many planners were sometimes also architects – look at John Madin's failed vision of Madeley, later Telford – told in a dreamy, ruminative, fictionalized way by Catherine O'Flynn in *The News Where You Are*. Madin's paymaster general in Birmingham was Herbert Manzoni, an engineer and the son of a sculptor who managed to push through a plethora of wild schemes that changed the face of the second city (though even he had a few plans he couldn't get past the Corporation). In an era where you could build an enormous ring road in Birmingham's city centre and erect dozens of brand-new towns in the English countryside, is it any wonder that planners were coming up with ever bigger and bolder schemes? They sniffed blood, sensed it was their time. So what if it never got built? It felt like it was the time to try. And even if not all of your proposals became reality (how many plans are left half-finished? – more than half, for sure) well, maybe you could get some of it built.

"After this, who believes in the idea of progress and perfectibility any more?"

ROBERT HUGHES ON LES TOURS AILLAUD, PARIS

The great unrealized plans of the twentieth century collapsed for many reasons. We reached the limits of our imaginations, the limits of our cheap energy supplies – as Barnabas Calder reminds us in *Architecture: From Prehistory to Climate Emergency* – and the limits of our ability to stomach top-down planning. 'By the 1970s, modern architecture long had been aligned with paradigms of top-down control, as much in evidence in Walter Gropius's appeals to "total architecture" as in Le Corbusier's sweeping plans for Paris, Algiers, and Rio de Janeiro,' says Todd Gannon in the introduction to the 2020 reprint of Reyner Banham's 1976 book *Megastructure*. 'At the same time, it [modern architecture] had come to symbolize the pursuit of emancipatory freedom from, among other things, the anachronisms of historical styles, the deprivations of the industrial city, and the oppressions of the bourgeois state.' Oscar Newman's interventions on the supposed anti-social, anti-human elements of modernism set the tone. Chris Morris nailed it in the satirical TV show *Brass Eye* in 1997, the 'Cowsick' sketch about a council estate blighted by 'git surfing' and youths who clogged up the gold mine vocalized the national mood – it was time to stop building anything 'public', and especially estates, because even if Paul McCartney donated 100 top hats to residents it would still be a failure.

Think of any major infrastructure scheme and the chances are there were protests against it: protest felled the Lower Manhattan Expressway (LOMEX) in New York and the Ringways scheme in London, and the Minnesota Experimental City; it very nearly did for Narita Airport in Japan and Mirabel Airport in Canada. Buckminster Fuller wanted to build a series of concave towers for the Skyrise project in Harlem; it was, though, the neighbourhood-focused ideas of J. Max Bond Jr, one of the few African-American architects anyone back then listened to, that came to represent the future in the East Harlem Triangle plan. How many non-white (or female) power brokers made big decisions? Very few indeed. No wonder word from on high was often unwelcome.

Adam Curtis's documentary series *The Century of the Self* showed how individualism triumphed as the twentieth century went on, how the collective went out of the window. This made it ever harder to get meaningful things built and it made modernism itself a kind of scapegoat. Yet it gave people the feeling that their lives were important and they should be listened to. This increased democratization empowered people to protest the powerful and disagree when they were told their house was being demolished for some new scheme or other. Curtis was also one of the first to point out the shoddiness of system building. Elsewhere it became increasingly obvious that 'construction = corruption' in many countries (not even just banana republics but, for example, Britain and Spain). Building itself got a bad rap.

Time moves so quickly these days that even those *grands projets* of the post-war era started coming down rapidly. Those buildings' threatened extinctions after such short lives (sometimes a paltry 20 or 30 years) intrigued people who developed an unexpected taste for the modernism in their cities and came out to try and save it from a very premature death, as with Birmingham's Central Library – part of the wider, unrealized Civic Centre plan for the city.

What about the idea of ambition – where did the dreamers go? In the twenty-first century there have been bold schemes, exciting architecture has been proposed. Today's radicals approach questions of what architecture should even be – like Assemble's ultra-democratic spaces and happenings. They are rooted in small communities. Bjarke Ingels still believes that he'll build on the moon one day. Fair play for having the balls to posit that. He told *Monocle* that 'Architecture is the art and science of turning fiction into fact.' As a novelist who writes books about architecture I look up to those that do the same thing better, like Jonathan Meades and Will Wiles, and hope, dear reader, that I'm delivering prose which will make you smile even if you don't consider it 'academic' enough. These fictions inevitably appeal to us because untrue stories in literature allow us to revel in fantastical worlds that take us outside our quotidian confines. The same goes with unbuilt architecture: would you prefer to look at a scheme for a Tesco with ten flats above it or one for a space station?

So what now? As I write, the greatest crisis of our (Western) lifetimes plays out (Syrians would take this banal apocalypse over being barrel-bombed every time, mind you); I cannot travel to explore any more urban archaeology because of lockdowns. By the time you hold this book in your hand this disgusting period – for do not let anyone convince you that we have gained anything from the trauma and disruption – will be a bad memory. I hope. Unfortunately, as with any stressful experience, the trauma will live on for years. Did we reach another point where, like at the tail end of the 1960s, we suffered a profound loss of confidence? Today's young architects could be scarred by the suffering, convincing themselves that 'to be modest' is the only (i.e. the only 'eco') answer. And maybe building itself will have become yet another undeserved pariah, like flying. Certainly fewer buildings have and will be built for a few years, yet even through the chaos the builders kept toiling; they were among the few who did.

Architecture works on long timelines – five years, sometimes more. Planning looks even further ahead – 10, 20, 30 years in the future. What will that future look like?

'Less is more,' said Mies van der Rohe. Then maybe nothing is even more. The most minimalist of all buildings is the one that simply doesn't exist – its walls so thin they are not visible, a preponderance of space and light as if there's nothing encasing you, no carbon footprint, totally sustainable and with aesthetics such that no one could possibly take a gander then take offence. The building that doesn't exist will always be perfect, never rot down, never let you down, never become a money pit. Maybe nothing is the future. From fantasizing about cities that never stop we could end up positing cities that never start.

But we must not lose faith in architecture as a symbol of what our short time on this planet represents: we cannot let ourselves become an epoch which leaves nothing to be discovered by future generations seeking information about the Second Dark Age of the 2020s. Architecture's ideas are its power; architecture's buildings are the promise writ large. Still, much will be unbuilt just like much has been unbuilt, and the study of what's not there, what should be there and what was meant to be there will enlighten and entertain as it does now. The dead can't speak to us, but we still read about them and we still write about them: they haunt us with their lack of presence, for ghosts exist only in the human mind (I think) and only because we want to connect to something (or someone). The obsession with plans, drawings, collages, remains hidden behind trees, and the obsession with theories themselves comes from that same place. What if. What if we had done something differently? Dreams pose the same points: a kiss with someone we never managed it with, a journey to a place destroyed by natural disaster, a poem spoken to a now dead parent. We had the ideas, we still have them; ideas are really all we have when all is said and done. They are what make us human. And if the wishes don't come true? Who cares. Keep going. Keep wishing. Keep dreaming. Until the end. And then ...? To sleep, perchance to dream.

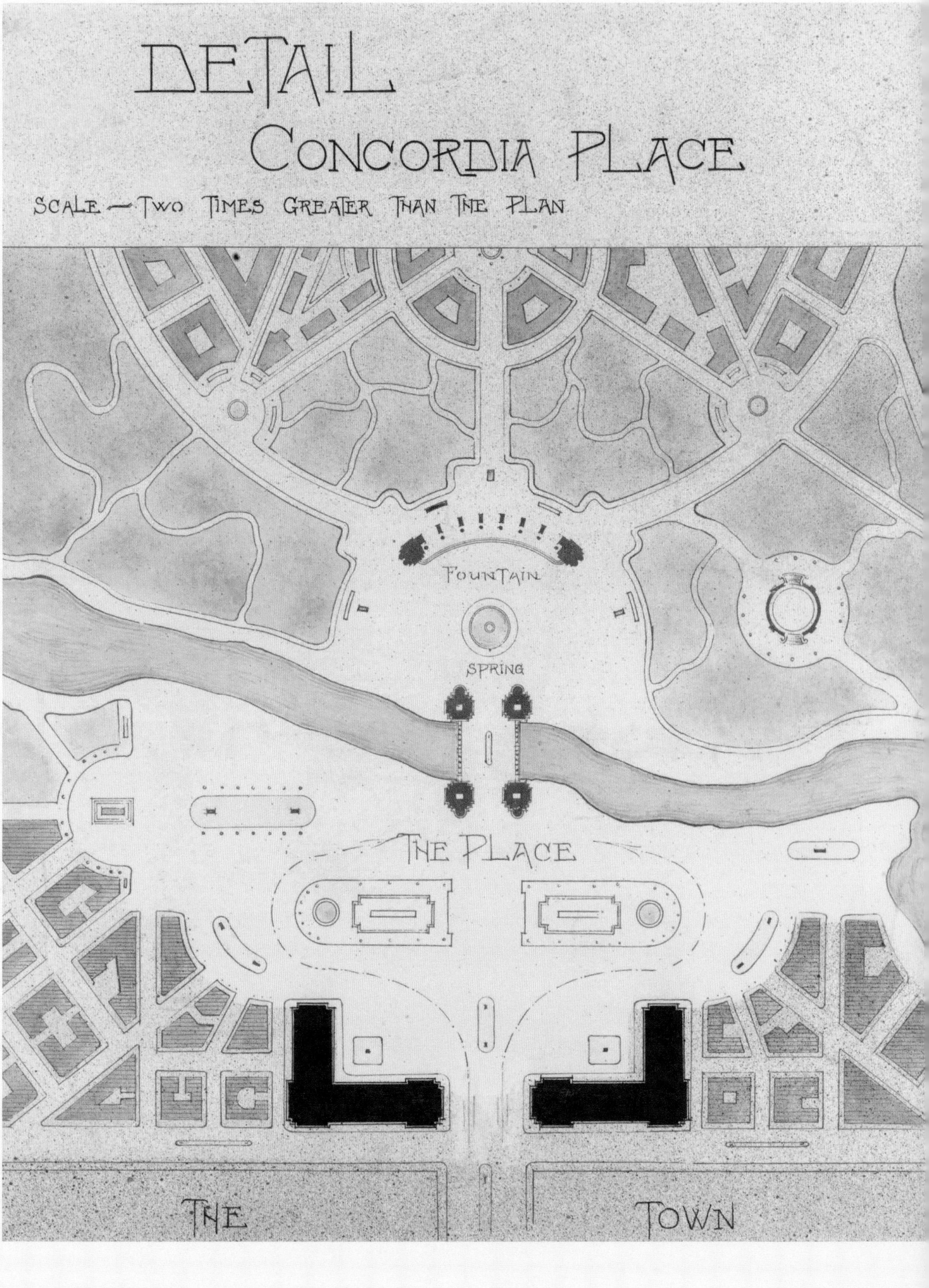
DETAIL
CONCORDIA PLACE
SCALE — TWO TIMES GREATER THAN THE PLAN
FOUNTAIN
SPRING
THE PLACE
THE
TOWN

POWER

‘Michelangelo was never so messed about by his Pope.’

PETER SMITHSON

BIRMINGHAM CIVIC CENTRE

BIRMINGHAM, UK 1940s-1970s

Birmingham's motto is 'Forward'. No other British city is so in thrall to progress. None so exuberantly destroyed its Victorian heritage in the twentieth century to build a future city, and none regretted it so much in the twenty-first, demolishing all that post-war innovation to rebuild yet again in a corporate style, which can be best described as being as bland as biscuits without any chocolate.

There were 1930s and 40s plans for a civic plaza with council buildings, cathedral and BBC studios. This led to the 1964 plan for a Civic Centre surrounding Centenary Square and strung out along the end of Broad Street – which is now more famous for piss-ups and punch-ups – called for student halls, a tower with a revolving restaurant, an exhibition centre (which one assumes would have been built instead of that favourite venue of the Conservative Party conference, the International Convention Centre), inevitably a monorail, flats, library, car parks, a sports academy, offices and even a planetarium. Everything would have linked by skyways. The exhibition halls and sky tower would be designed by James Roberts and the rest by John Madin. In the event the library was built by 1974 (Madin and John Ericsson as job architect) and became something of an icon – the library was the silent fulcrum around which the motorway madness swirled.

But most of the plans, including water gardens, never materialized, and a slightly forlorn library was pulled down in 2015. Much of my novel *The Wall in the Head* takes place where the Civic Centre was due to stand, at the library and where Alpha Tower and the studios for the local ITV concession ATV were built instead of the exhibition centre and sky tower. Across the city, next to New Street Station, James Roberts's Rotunda still stands, and in fact you can stay in one of its rooms – in 2008 it reopened after conversion from offices to residential, including a hotel with the best views over Birmingham.

PREVIOUS PAGE Concordia Place, part of Alfred Agache's 1912 designs for Canberra, Australia.

LEFT John Madin with his model for the 1960s Birmingham Civic Centre.

Birmingham Central Library.

Salads Sandwiches Pasta Smoothies

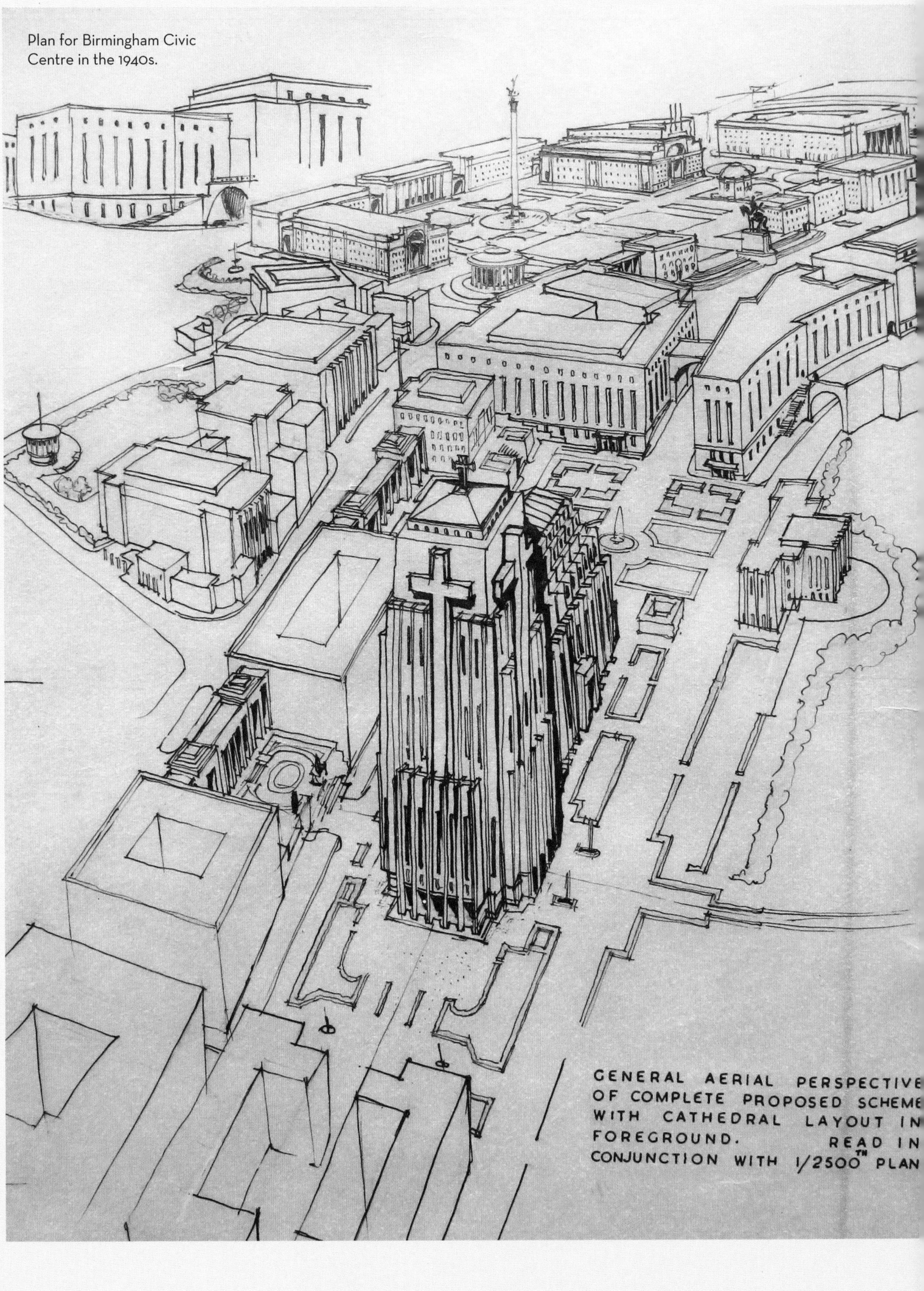
GENERAL AERIAL PERSPECTIVE
OF COMPLETE PROPOSED SCHEME
WITH CATHEDRAL LAYOUT IN
FOREGROUND. READ IN
CONJUNCTION WITH 1/2500TH PLAN

Plan for Birmingham Civic Centre in the 1940s.

Birmingham Central Library was one part of the Civic Centre plan realized in 1974 and since demolished.

THE BRUCE PLAN

GLASGOW, UK 1945

Optimism. We forget that the twentieth century was full of it. Perhaps because the dystopian narrative is more compelling. The picture of crazed lunatics in town planning offices with the gall to knock down half of a city and replace it with tower blocks is the image that recurs; it's the stick used to beat all of the philosophies that went with modernism.

In many senses Robert Bruce's 1945 plan for Glasgow was brutal. Knocking down Charles Rennie Mackintosh's School of Art (plus many, many other historic edifices) – really? But the thinking was this: create a modern city fit for purpose; house poor people in better conditions; and preserve Glasgow as a great socialist industrial city.

Central government in the UK has long been suspicious of 'red cities' with too much power. They want to keep Birmingham, Newcastle and Glasgow from being too troublesome. One way to do this is to hobble their huge, Labour-dominated city councils (city-states, really) by promoting decentralization – so the population disperses to the countryside, county towns and new towns. In 1945, Glasgow was really trying to keep the maximum amount of people and industry inside its boundaries; to reinvent itself by building high and building modern. Bruce's view was just more radical than almost anywhere else in the UK. But, like many other plans of the time, it was about removing filth and disorder and poverty from cities – to make them thrive again. Not that he asked anyone living there what they wanted; that approach only came much later in the century.

Bruce wanted to redesign and rebuild almost the entire city centre. Straight streets, rectilinear blocks, motorways. He also wanted to bin the terrible tenements and house the workers from the Highlands, from Ireland, from Italy, from Lithuania, in big new estates.

So how did the story end? The housing estates got built, as did many of the motorways – the M8 was dropped on to Glasgow's city centre like a doughnut into hot fat. It was unwanted, and yet ... You get a great sense of drama driving along it, ploughing right into the city's core.

The city centre was partly redeveloped on a block-by-block basis, and on a bigger scale, with huge, odd precincts of offices and shops, and bus stands at Anderston. But mostly the city centre, with its Victorian sandstone and art deco, survived. Now it's a regular stand-in location for New York in movies and a home to boutique shops.

Glasgow, in a way, got the best of both worlds. History preserved in the very centre, fascinating newness on the fringes. It remains one of the most exciting-looking cities in the UK. The optimism fizzled away though. From the heady days of propaganda films like *Glasgow 1980* – with the funkiest soundtrack this side of Harlem and edited by *Gregory's Girl* and *That Sinking Feeling* director Bill Forsyth – and a belief in the future embodied in Basil Spence's Hutchesontown flats in the Gorbals (opened by the Queen but now demolished), we ended up with Andrea Arnold's 2006 film *Red Road*, set in the eponymous and now also demolished flats in the north-east of the city.

From utopia to dystopia in half a century. Yet Glasgow's innovations during that period should also be remembered: its housing, its bold motorway designs, its cheap-and-cheerful concrete universities and colleges, and its big plans to keep people away from heavy industry yet preserve jobs. Most of all, the city was trying to save itself during some tough times.

Map of new street layouts and neighbourhoods in Central Glasgow as outlined in Robert Bruce's plan.

THE CORPORATION OF THE CITY OF GLASGOW.

Folio No.—8

FIRST PLANNING REPORT

INNER CORE OF THE CITY

MODIFICATION OF EXISTING ROAD SYSTEM

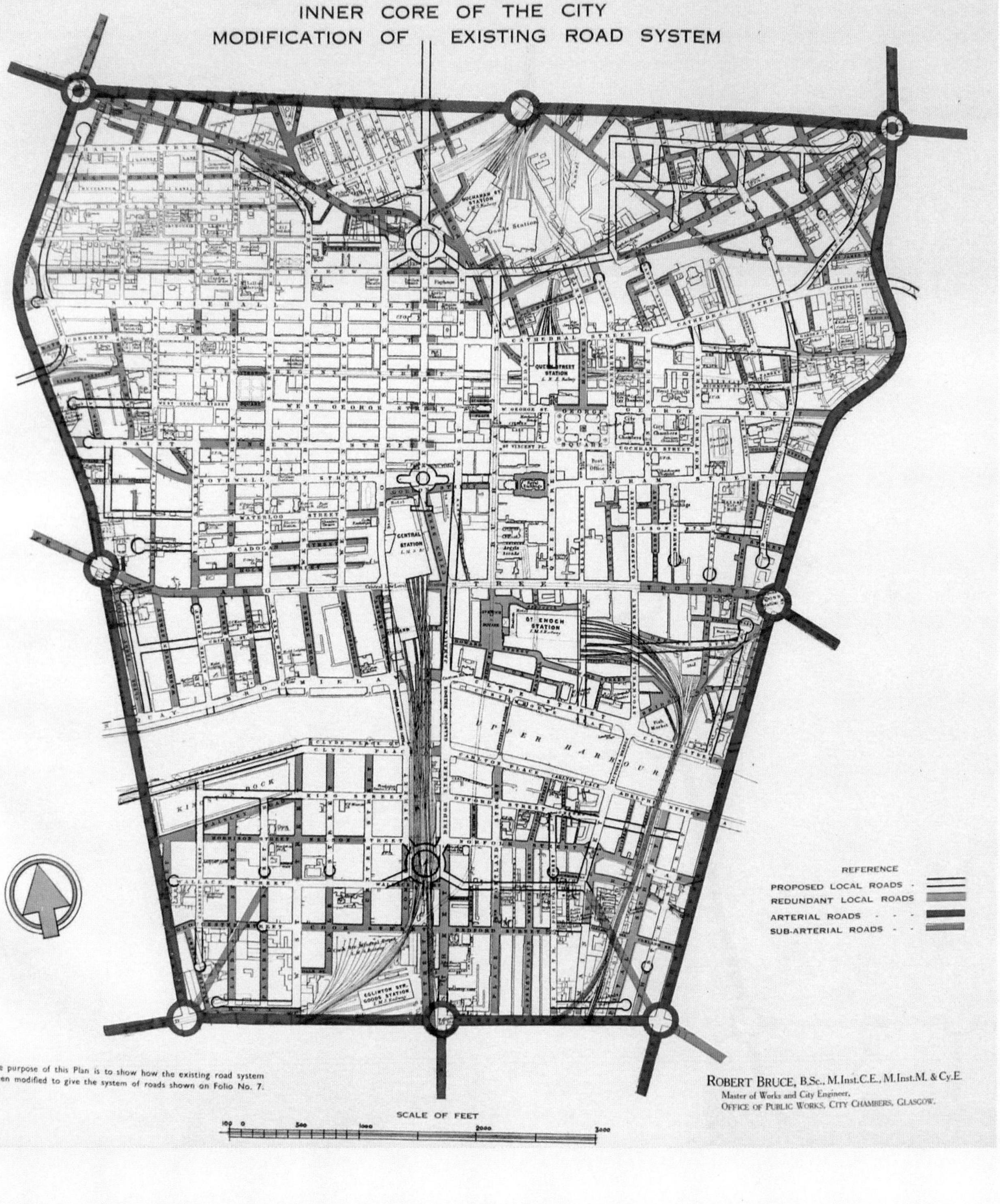

The purpose of this Plan is to show how the existing road system s been modified to give the system of roads shown on Folio No. 7.

ROBERT BRUCE, B.Sc., M.Inst.C.E., M.Inst.M. & Cy.E.
Master of Works and City Engineer,
OFFICE OF PUBLIC WORKS, CITY CHAMBERS, GLASGOW.

PITTSBURGH CIVIC CENTER

PITTSBURGH, USA 1947

Nowadays, entrepreneurs and designers of all stripes like to boast about their green credentials – even if those credentials can sometimes seem a little forced. But back in 1930s America, the environment wasn't exactly the number-one concern anywhere. Frank Lloyd Wright was an architect who did care about nature, who wanted to realize some kind of accommodation between buildings and the natural world in which they sat. But he never quite found the sweet spot, and his architecture constantly pulled in opposing directions.

Did he hate 'the city'? Probably. He certainly wanted to live out in the sun and the peace of Arizona, and his most famous building, Fallingwater, a house in the middle of nowhere, seems to

RIGHT Plan for Pittsburgh showing Point Park and the Twin Bridges at night.

BELOW Frank Lloyd Wright.

Plan for Frank Lloyd Wright's Twin Bridges project.

effortlessly blend concrete with conifers, ribbed steel with rivers. He, like many Americans at that time, believed in the suburbs as the future and the car as the vehicle for that monumental social change.

All these contradictions and complexities came to a head in Wright's most startling unrealized vision: an enormous civic centre for downtown Pittsburgh, a rough-and-ready steelmaking city.

In the 1930s the city wanted to regenerate the wastelands at the meeting of its two rivers – a site of unparalleled natural beauty with hills overlooking the meeting of the waters, but one which had been scarred by industry. After the Second World War a victorious and confident America looked to a future where it could do anything. And it was from this optimism that, in 1947, Wright's Point Park plan emerged: a thumping megastructure right in the middle of Pittsburgh, set between the city's bridges. Towers would surround the main structure, which would house offices, leisure and entertainment venues, while a spiralling car ramp encased the building.

The plan was commissioned by Edgar Kaufmann, a Pittsburgh retailer for whom Wright had built Fallingwater a hundred miles away. It was bold, brazen – but never built. A later Wright plan saw an altered vision – a tower, but no superstructure and a park instead. That too never took off.

Instead, today there's a more modest park at the confluence point and various shops and offices around the edge of the site, but nothing as monumental as Wright suggested; though he probably would have liked the park.

In the original plan we see Wright's conflicts bubble to the surface: as in many of his visions there was a rooftop park (today's skyscrapers almost always feature 'sky gardens' and 'green roofs', indebted to FLW) yet there was also roaring car traffic on that ramp. It was a plan to reinvigorate a city yet it would have made the city noisy, smelly and unwalkable – and essentially easy to escape from by car. Most US city design from 1920 to 1990 was based on this premise of easy egress, to your suburban house many miles away.

But Wright's vision didn't fade entirely, and the shape of the ramps on the superstructure lives on famously in something else we all know and love: New York's Guggenheim Museum, built in 1959. It looks like a veritable cake served at afternoon tea when compared to FLW's jarringly, crashingly modern Pittsburgh plan.

LOS ANGELES CIVIC CENTER

LOS ANGELES, USA 1925

Frank Lloyd Wright's attempt to build a new civic centre for Los Angeles was never going to fly. LA's chief monument is its freeways (they came later than the 1925 proposal from FLW for new government buildings) and those freeways allowed the city to develop in a most un-urban manner. Dislocated suburbs grew in a piecemeal fashion and *grands projets* never really seemed to materialize. The freeways also made the centre redundant – like the hole in a doughnut, as Jonathan Meades pointed out when discussing Britain's answer to an American motor city, Birmingham. Lloyd Wright's avenue stacked with a brash, obese, deco-ish ensemble of buildings is overbearing; you can even see something of the horror of Germania in its overblown monumentality.

FLW did eventually get to design a government complex – though he died before it was built – at the other end of the state in Marin County. That lower-rise campus surrounded by parkland came in 1962, anticipating the Silicon Valley tech HQs obsessively arrayed around natural features, despite their output being the very opposite of nature. Marin County Civic Centre starred in George Lucas's 1971 filmic dystopia *THX 1138*.

ALTERNATIVE PLANS FOR CANBERRA

CANBERRA, AUSTRALIA 1912

At the deadline of the 1912 competition to design a new Australian capital, 137 entries had come in. The ideas for the 'bush capital' were varied, from high modernism to bucolic arts and crafts. Runners-up included local lads Walter Scott Griffiths, Robert Charles Coulter and Charles Henry Caswell, who went for a series of straight avenues and monumental buildings, Eliel Saarinen – who chucked down a vision of almost what a Soviet city on the water such as Minsk looks like – and Alfred Agache, who submitted a kind of 3D map of a theme park with different-coloured zones and snakey connections between the clumps of trees. Walter Burley Griffin is always cited as the competition winner but this is typically sexist – it was his wife Marion Mahony Griffin who was much of the brains behind this proposal, having earned her stripes under Frank Lloyd Wright. Many of the original elements of the Griffins' plan were never constructed.

And many changes in the direction of the city never happened: not least the idea of a raised deck down by the lake which would have been the home of the new Parliament and many other public buildings in the 1960s. This plan was nixed, the Parliament was built up the hill, and the extant late modernist buildings by the shore of Lake Burley Griffin – notably the National Gallery of Australia – were left with disconnected upper-floor access, platforms, stairs and stubs which would have connected onto the raised plaza and walkways that were never achieved.

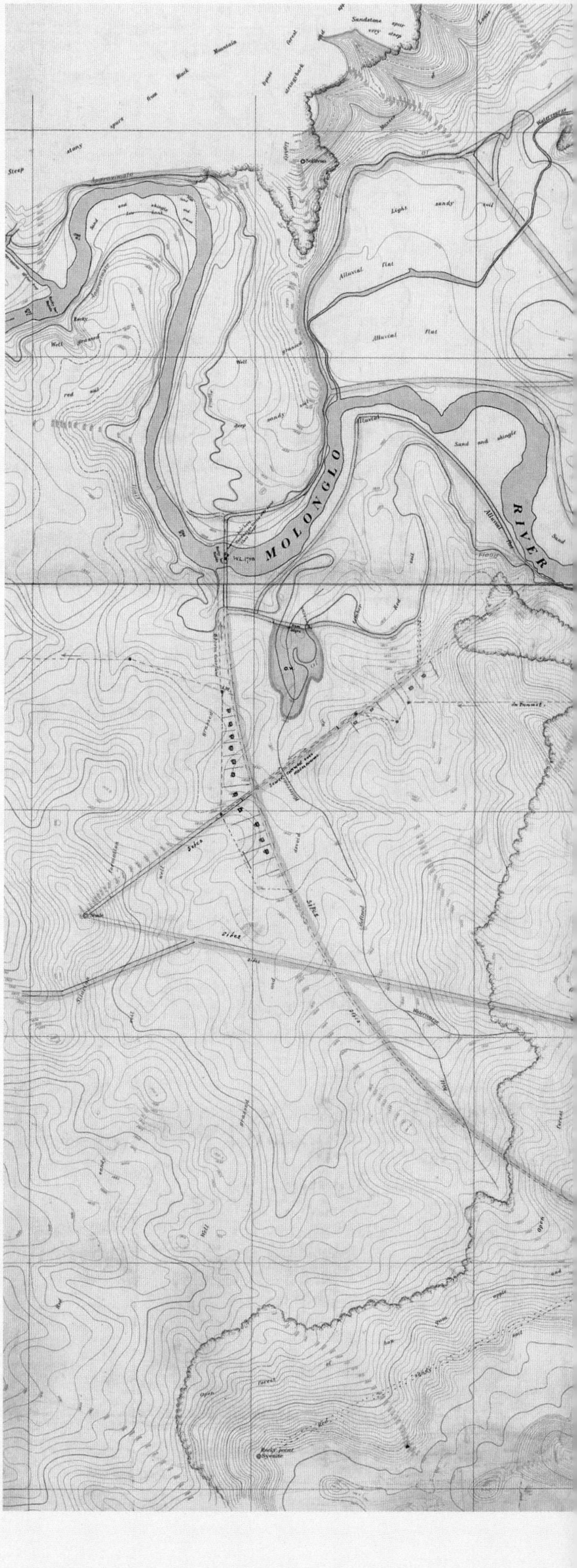

The proposed plan for the site for the federal capital of Australia: map of a contour survey of the site by George Wilson.

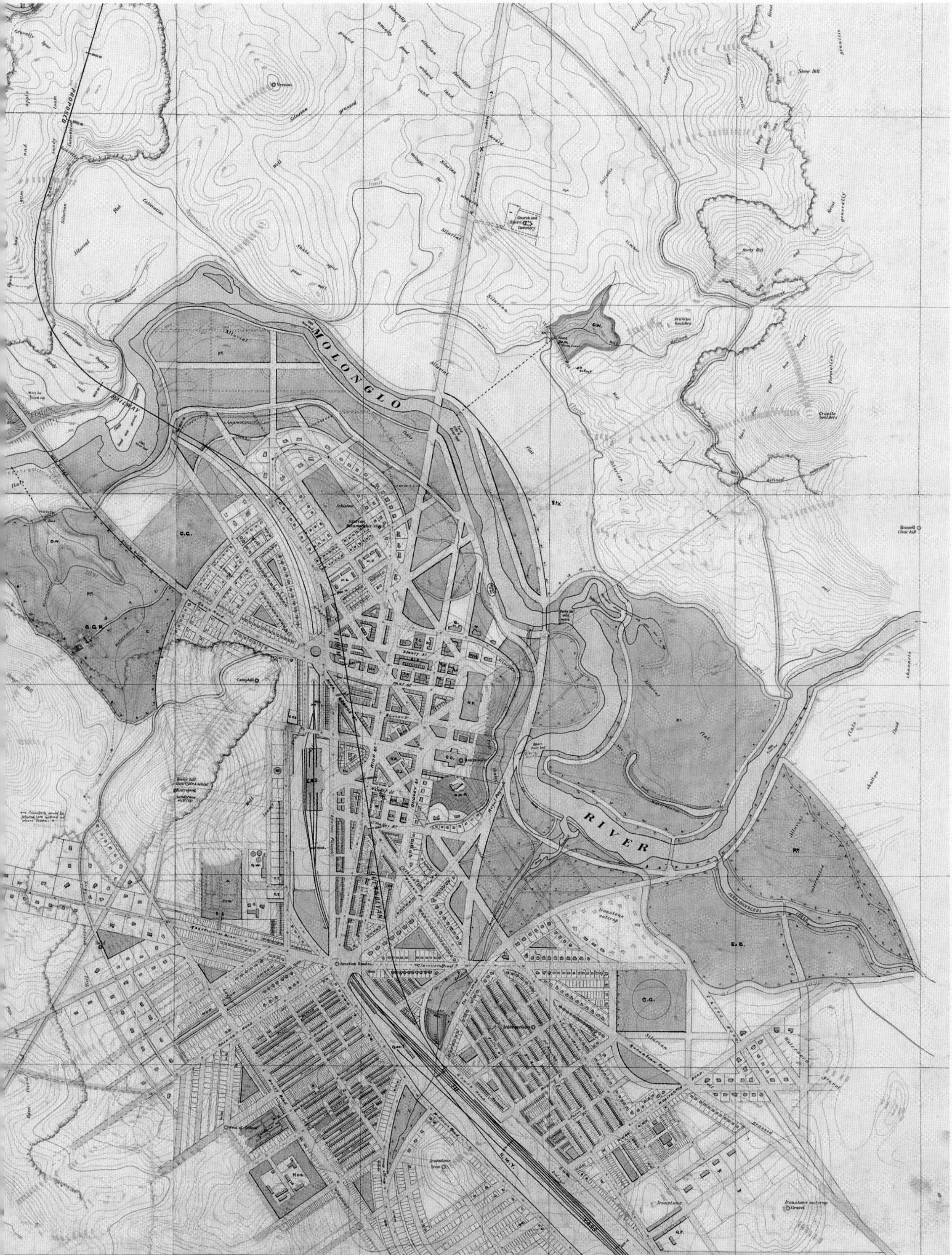
MOLONGLO
RIVER
Stony Hill
Rocky Hill
C.G.

PLAN
OF
THE PROPOSED
FEDERAL CAPITAL
OF
AUSTRALIA
Flats & Shop Areas indicated thus
Rows of Houses for single Families shown thus
Private Villas & Semidetached Dwellings thus

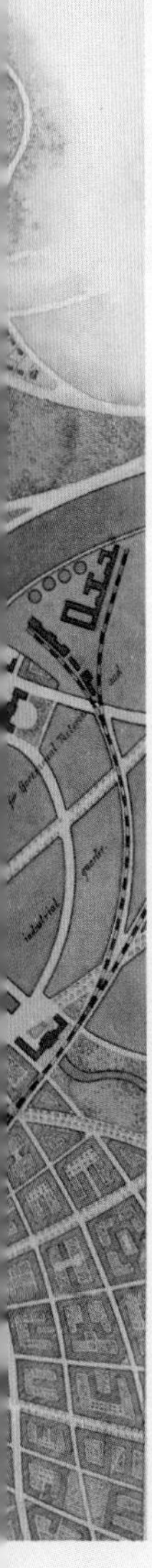

ABOVE Eliel Saarinen's idea for the Australian House of Parliament and lake.

OPPOSITE Saarinen's plan to build the city of Canberra.

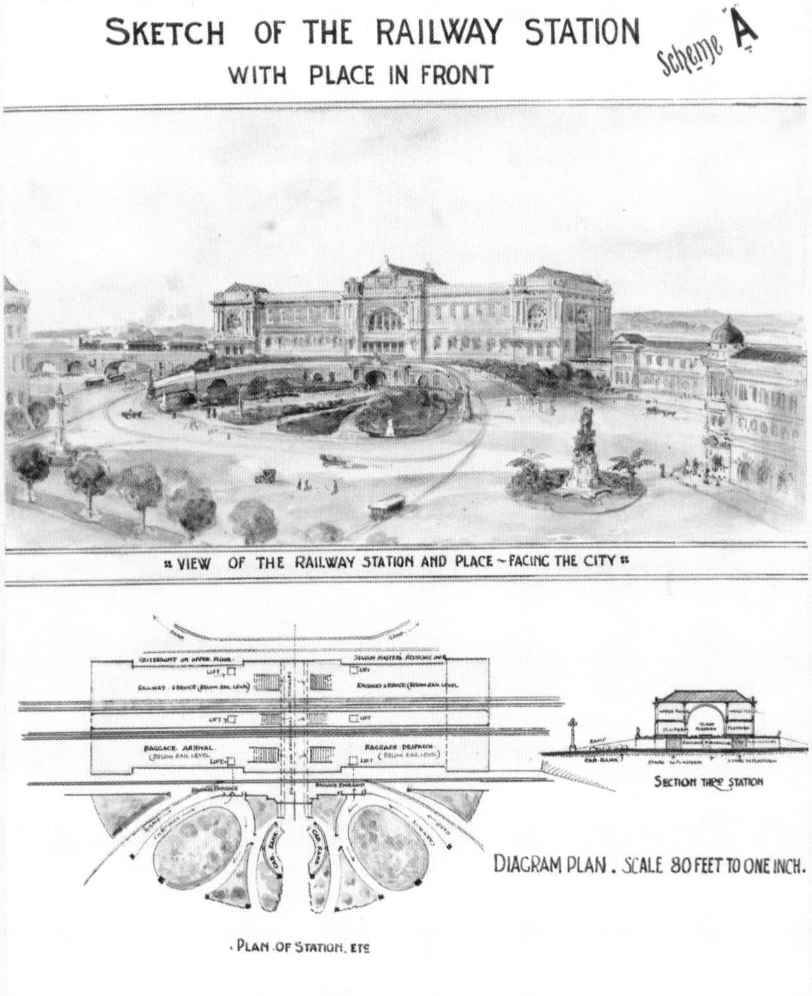

RIGHT Walter Scott Griffiths, Robert Charles Coulter and Charles Henry Caswell's plan for Canberra's railway station.

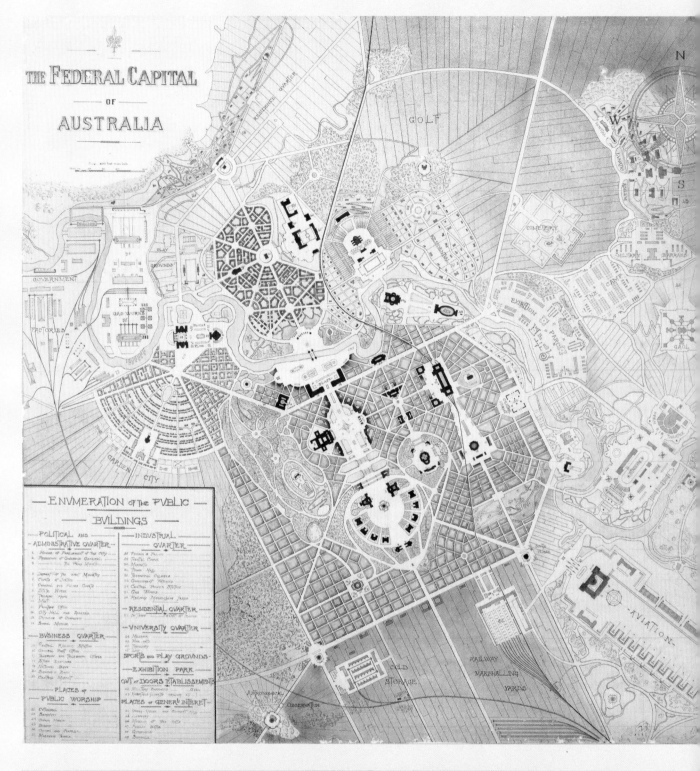

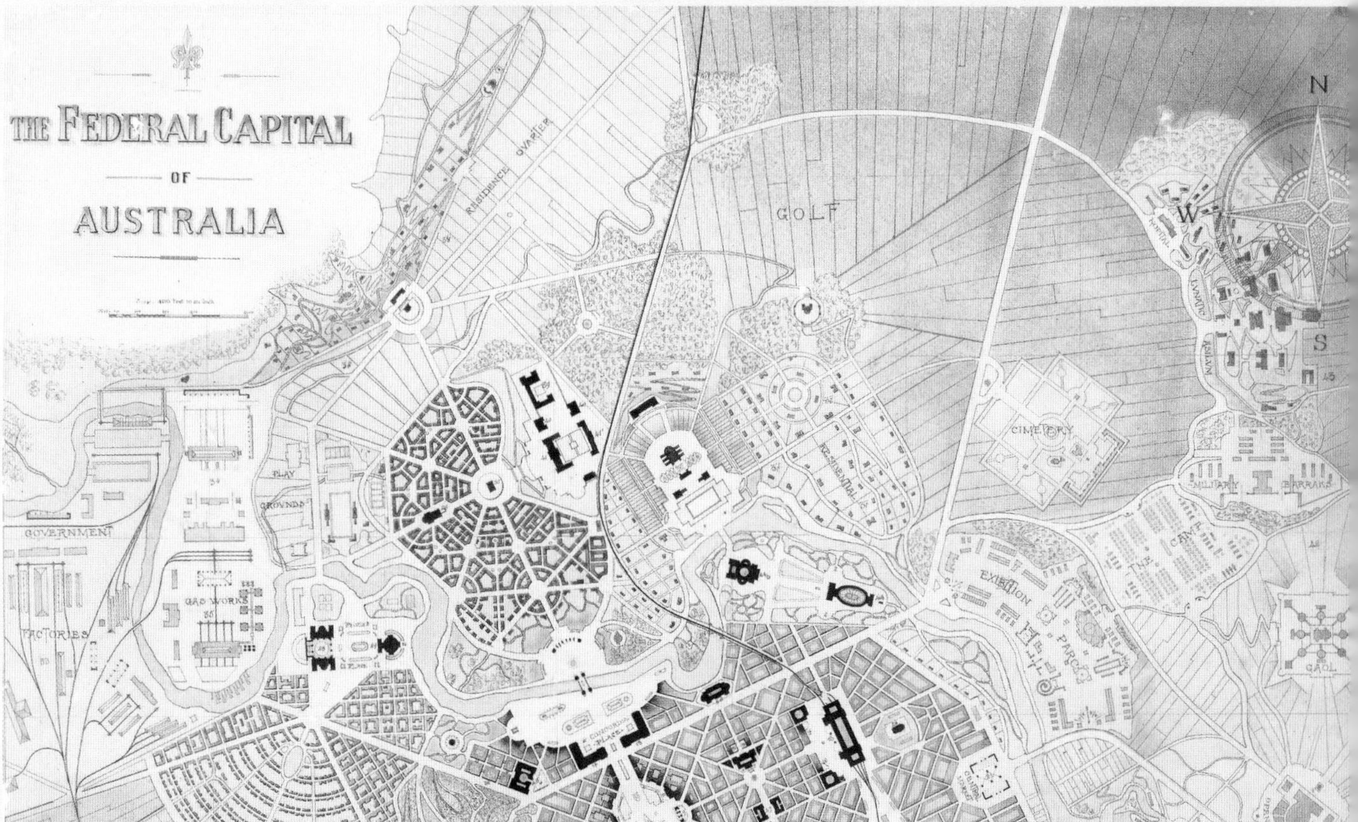
THE FEDERAL CAPITAL
OF
AUSTRALIA
GOLF
RESIDENTIAL QUARTER
PLAY GROUNDS
GOVERNMENT
FACTORIES
GAS WORKS
CIMETERY
MILITARY BARRACKS
CAMP
EXHIBITION PARK
GAOL
GARDEN CITY
THEATER
AVIATION
COLD STORAGE
RAILWAY MARSHALLING YARDS
ASTRONOMICAL OBSERVATION
N
W
S
ENUMERATION OF THE PUBLIC BUILDINGS
POLITICAL AND ADMINISTRATIVE QUARTER
INDUSTRIAL QUARTER
RESIDENTIAL QUARTER
UNIVERSITY QUARTER
BUSINESS QUARTER
SPORTS AND PLAY GROUNDS
EXHIBITION PARK
OUT OF DOORS ETABLISSEMENTS
PLACES OF PUBLIC WORSHIP
PLACES OF GENERAL INTERET

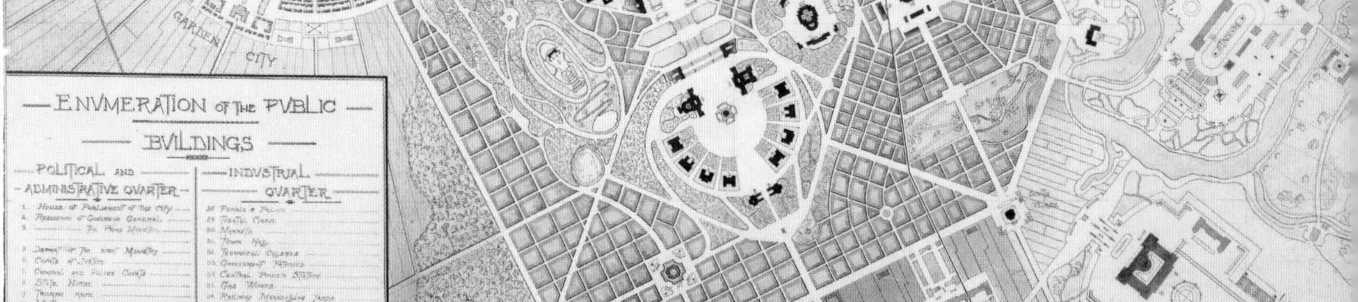
ON BOARD AN AEROPLAN
AT A HEIGHT OF 3280 FEET
VIEW TAKEN FROM A
OF 24000 FEET

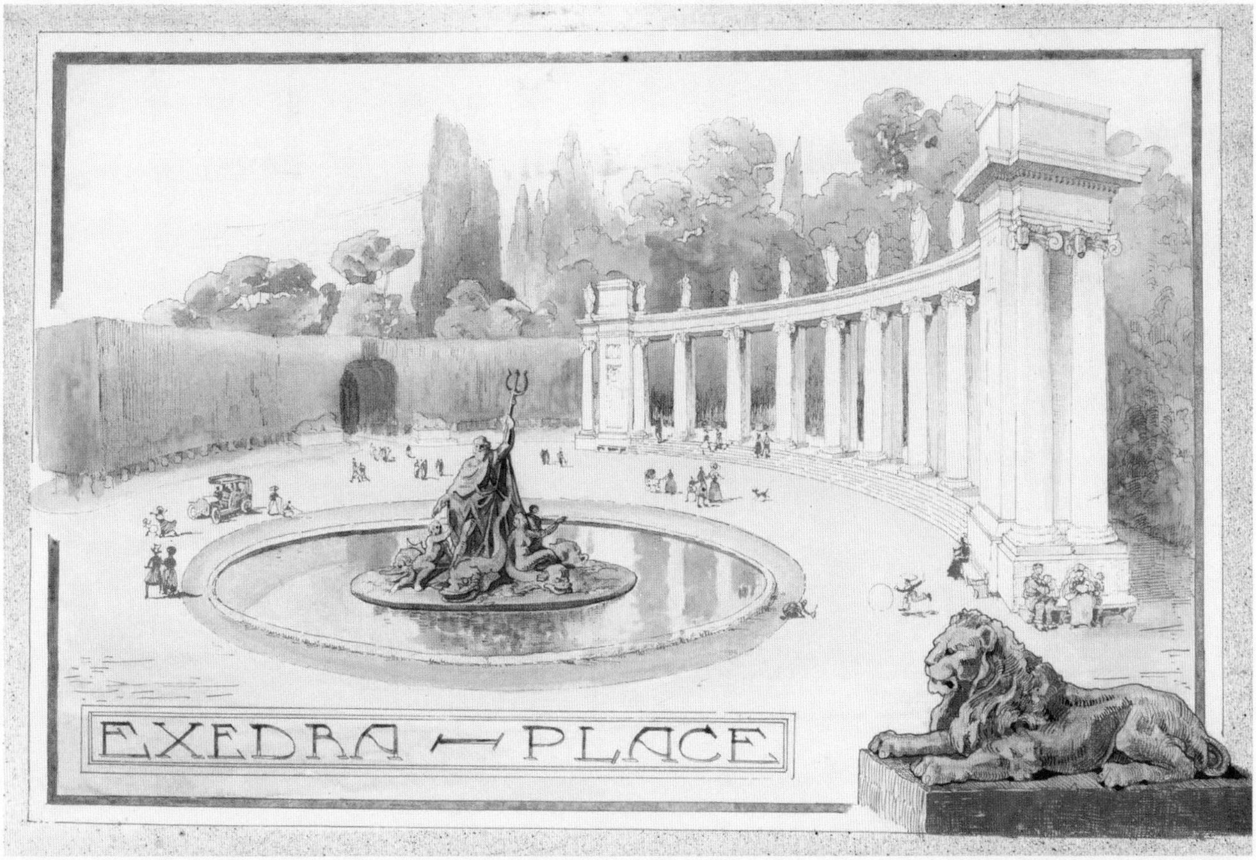

OPPOSITE, ABOVE Alfred Agache's plan for Canberra.

OPPOSITE, BELOW Alfred Agache's plan as viewed from the air.

TOP Drawing of Exedra Place by Alfred Agache.

ABOVE Perspective of the proposed People's Palace by Alfred Agache.

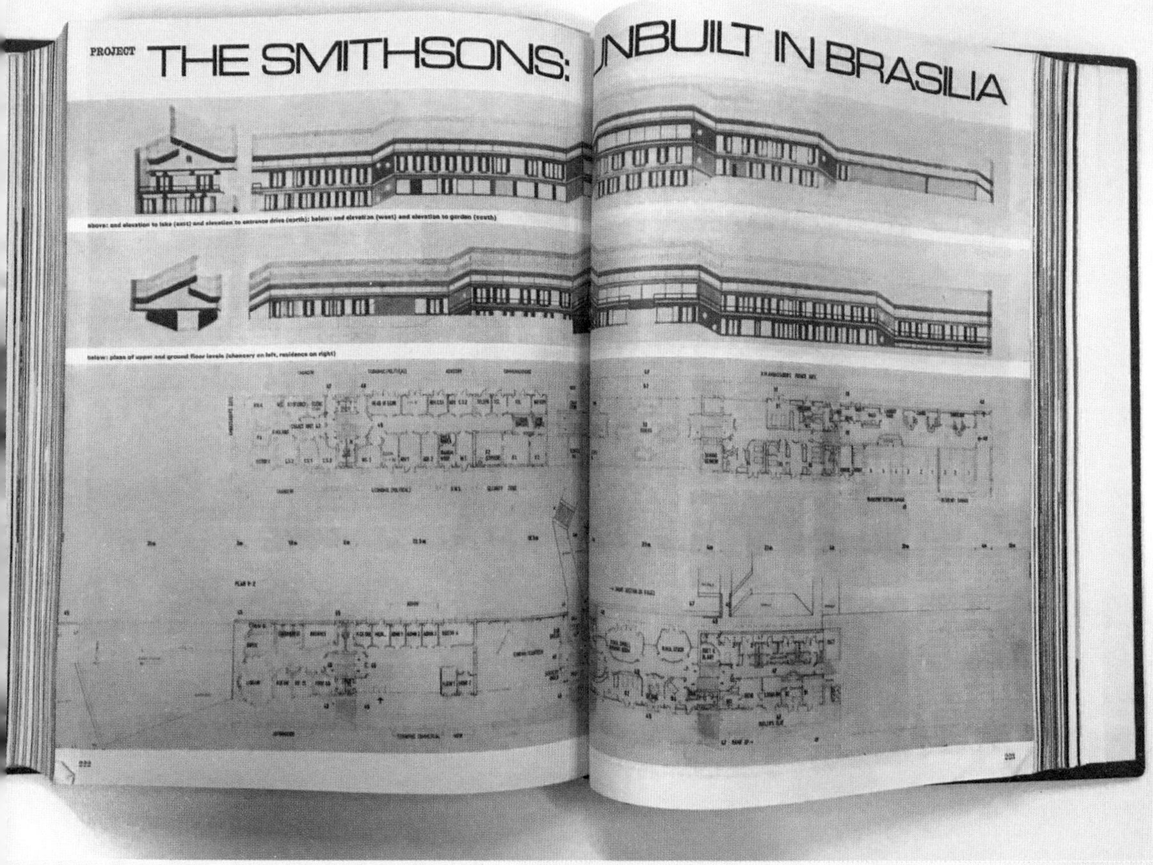

Plan for the British Embassy, Brasilia, featured in the *Architectural Review*, 1975.

BRITISH EMBASSY, BRASILIA

BRASILIA, BRAZIL 1965

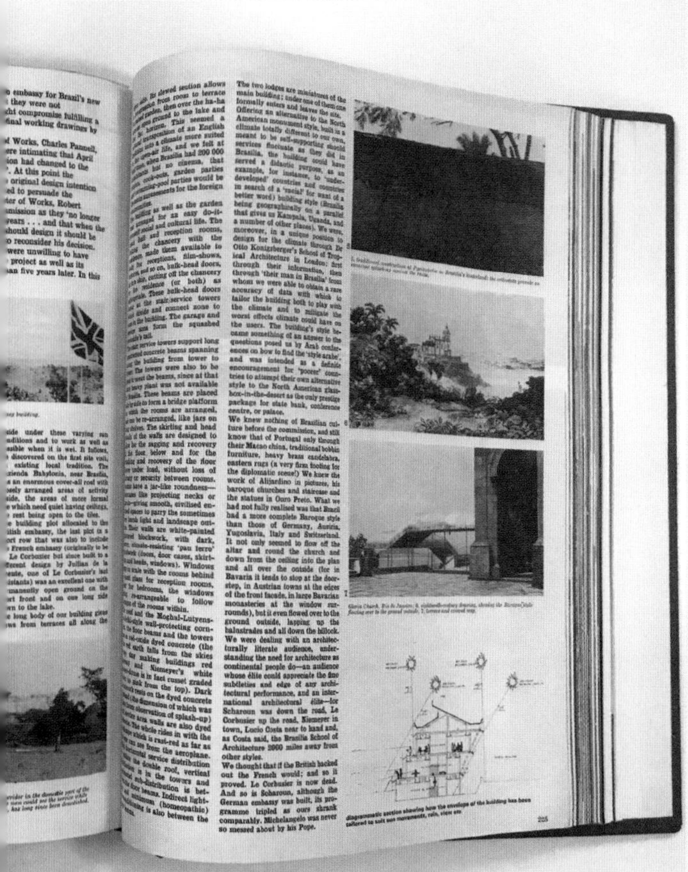

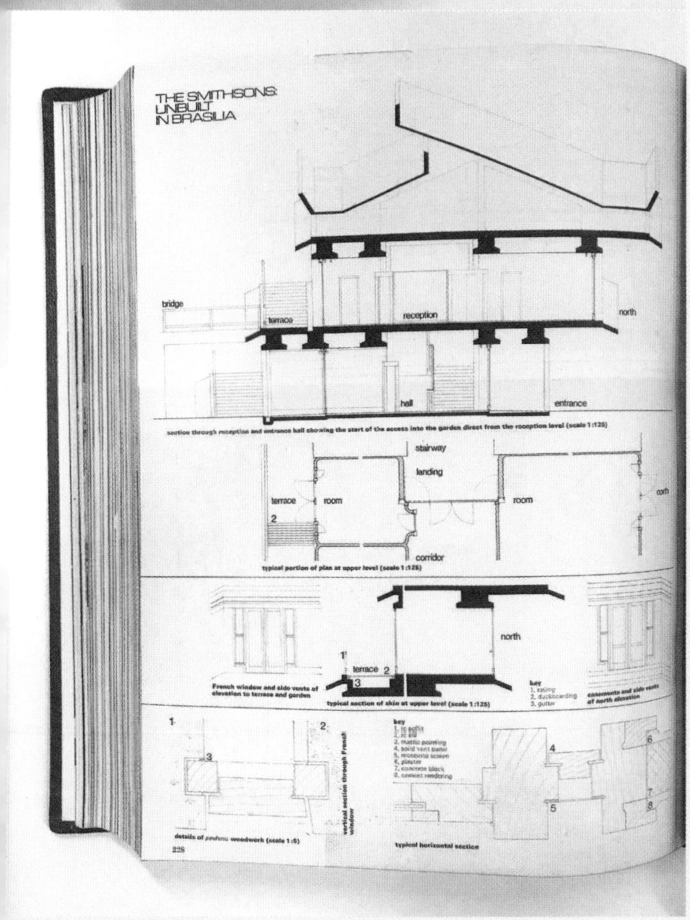

Alison and Peter Smithson were no strangers to unrealized projects. These two 'pamphleteers', as Jonathan Meades jokes, were to be found lecturing, making exhibitions, appearing in iconic photos, wearing silvery space uniforms from the future and taking part in the near-legendary *The Smithsons on Housing*, a BBC documentary which, as Jonathan Coe explains in the best biography you'll ever read, sank the nascent directing career of the writer B.S. Johnson. Plans for Berlin and Sheffield University and Golden Lane in London evaporated, the Coventry Cathedral gig went to Basil Spence.

And then Brasilia: their 1965 plan for a 'squashed crocodile' would have provided the embassy and ambassador's house by the lakeside, with a building open to gardens and even, yes, a haha. Peter wrote in the *Architectural Review* retrospectively in 1975: 'This seemed a natural transposition of an English tradition into a climate more suited to the open-air life.' They didn't patronize their audience (they didn't compromise either): 'We were dealing with an architecturally literate audience, understanding the need for architecture as continental people do,' continued Peter.

UK government dithering and cost-cutting sank the project. The 'continentals' couldn't manage much better: Le Corbusier was to design the French embassy to Brazil next door, but this was scrapped too. This, despite the richness of modern architecture in the city. It was not a richness that charmed everyone, though: Robert Hughes called it 'a ceremonial slum' and flew straight home to New York in disgust.

GERMANIA

BERLIN, GERMANY 1938-42

Right off General-Pape-Strasse, not far from the former airport at Tempelhof, I find Berlin's oddest *denkmal*, or memorial. In a city of weirdness this is surely eccentric – a massive concrete block the shape of a biscuit tin, surrounded by bushes next to a normal Kreuzberg apartment block. I climb the ladder to a viewing platform and look down on the last vestige of Welthauptstadt Germania, Adolf Hitler and Albert Speer's disgraceful plan to venerate the genocidal state – after its assumed victory over everyone – and its corporate apologists with a neo-classical super-city that would have included a venue (the Volkshalle) so large that audiences breathing would have created their own internal weather.

The Schwerbelastungskörper – meaning 'heavy load-bearing object' – was installed here to see if Berlin's wet, flat ground could take the heaviness of this physical pomp – specifically the triumphal arch. Any idiot could have told you what the engineers eventually did: of course it could not. The triumphal arch and the huge buildings each side of the ceremonial North–South Axis would have sunk, and luckily so did the National Socialist regime. This block remains – too heavy, too bulky, too near the railway tracks south to Leipzig to be blown up or removed – as a physical reminder of megalomania's murky limits. A museum is attached telling the story of the concentration camp prisoners sacrificed in the quarries to cut the granite.

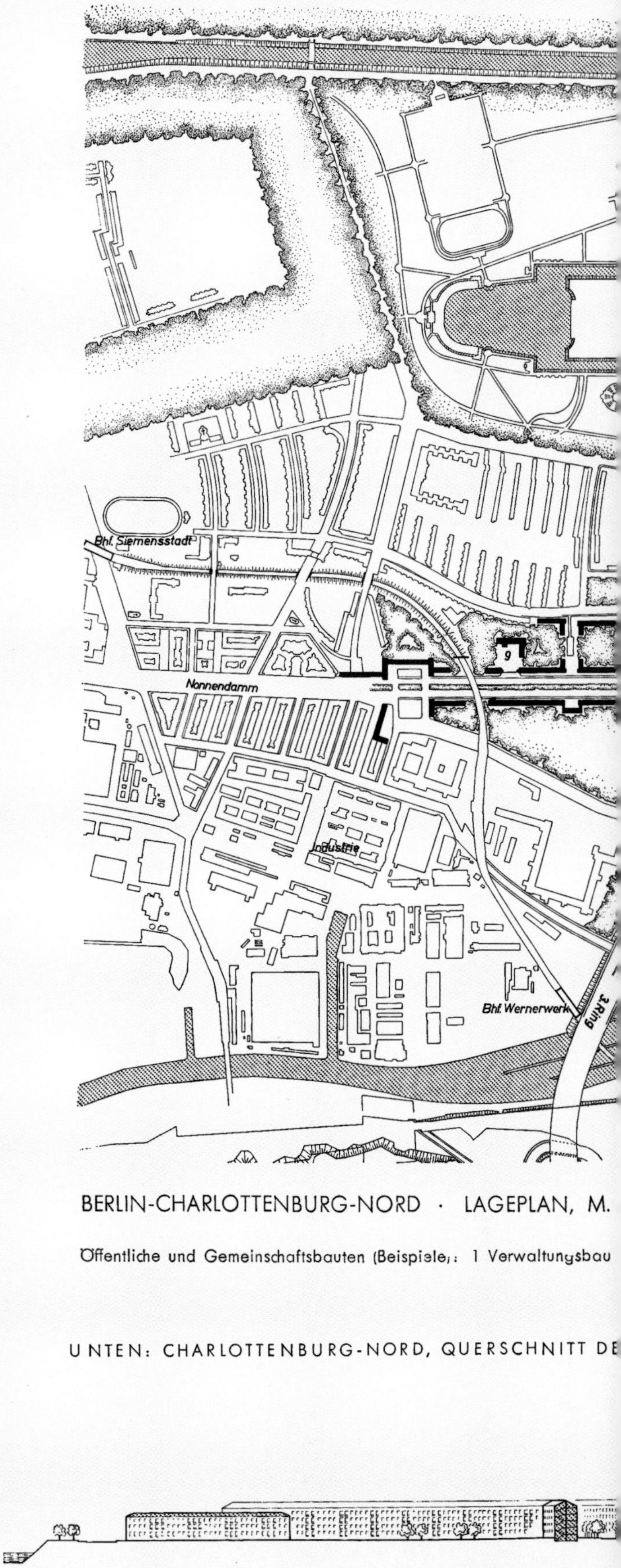

RIGHT Charlottenburg-North and Jungfernheide Park Plan by Albert Speer.

OVERLEAF, LEFT Planning of ring roads and an East-West and North-South axis for Berlin.

OVERLEAF, RIGHT Germania top view: drafts by Albert Speer from the late 1930s.

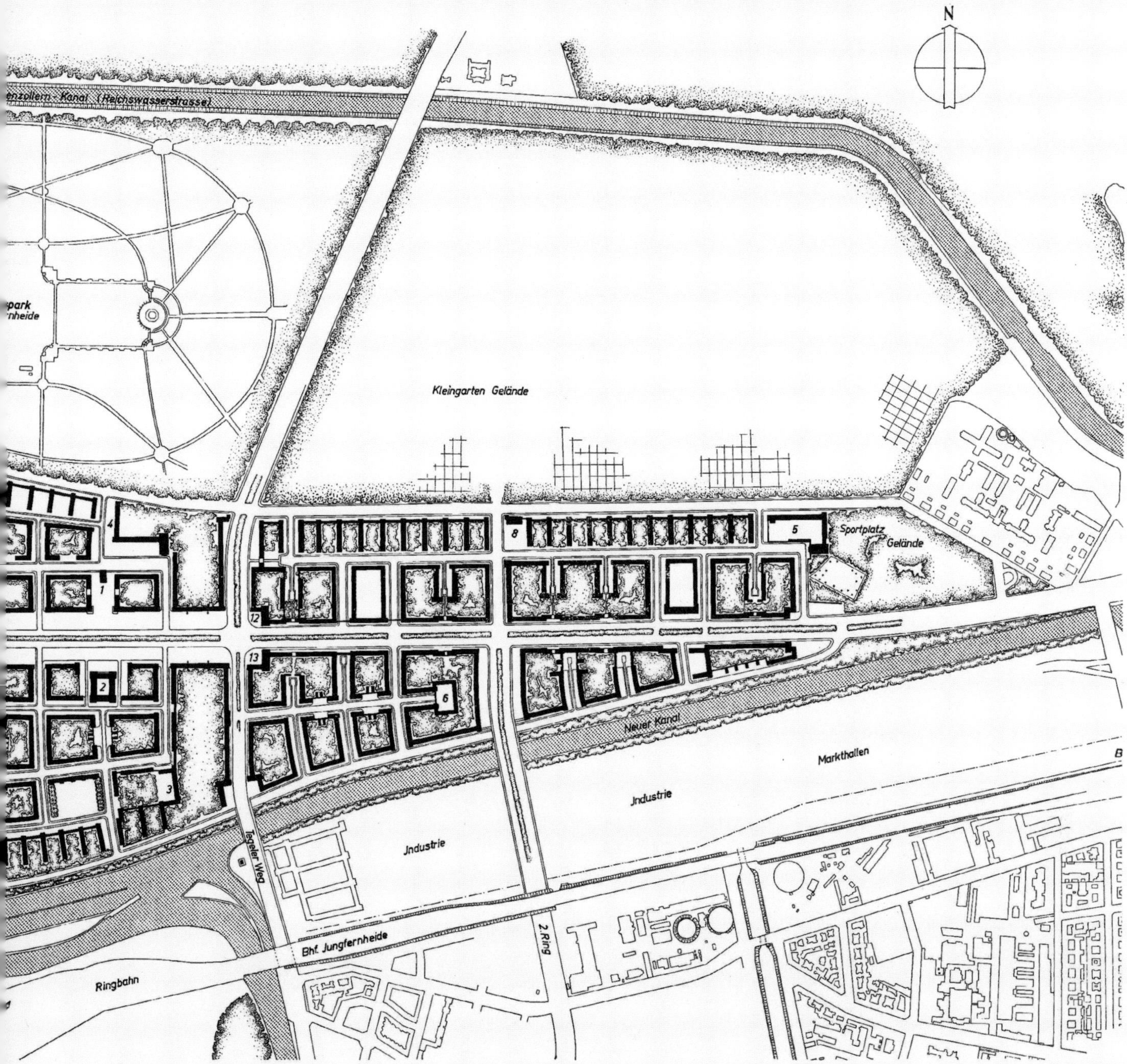

WURF: STÄDTISCHES HAUPTPLANUNGSAMT UNTER LEITUNG DES GENERALBAUINSPEKTORS FÜR DIE REICHSHAUPTSTADT

le 4 HJ.-Heim 5 HJ.-Heim 6 Kindertagesstätten 7 Altersheim 8 Kirche 9 Feuerwehr 10 Kaffeehaus 11 Gaststätte 12 Postamt 13 Polizei 14 Lichtspielhaus

UUNG IN NORD-SÜD-RICHTUNG, M. 1:3000

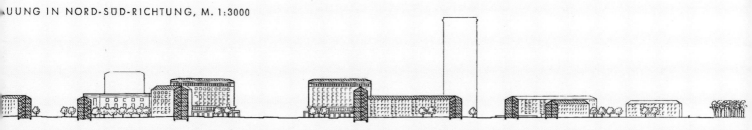

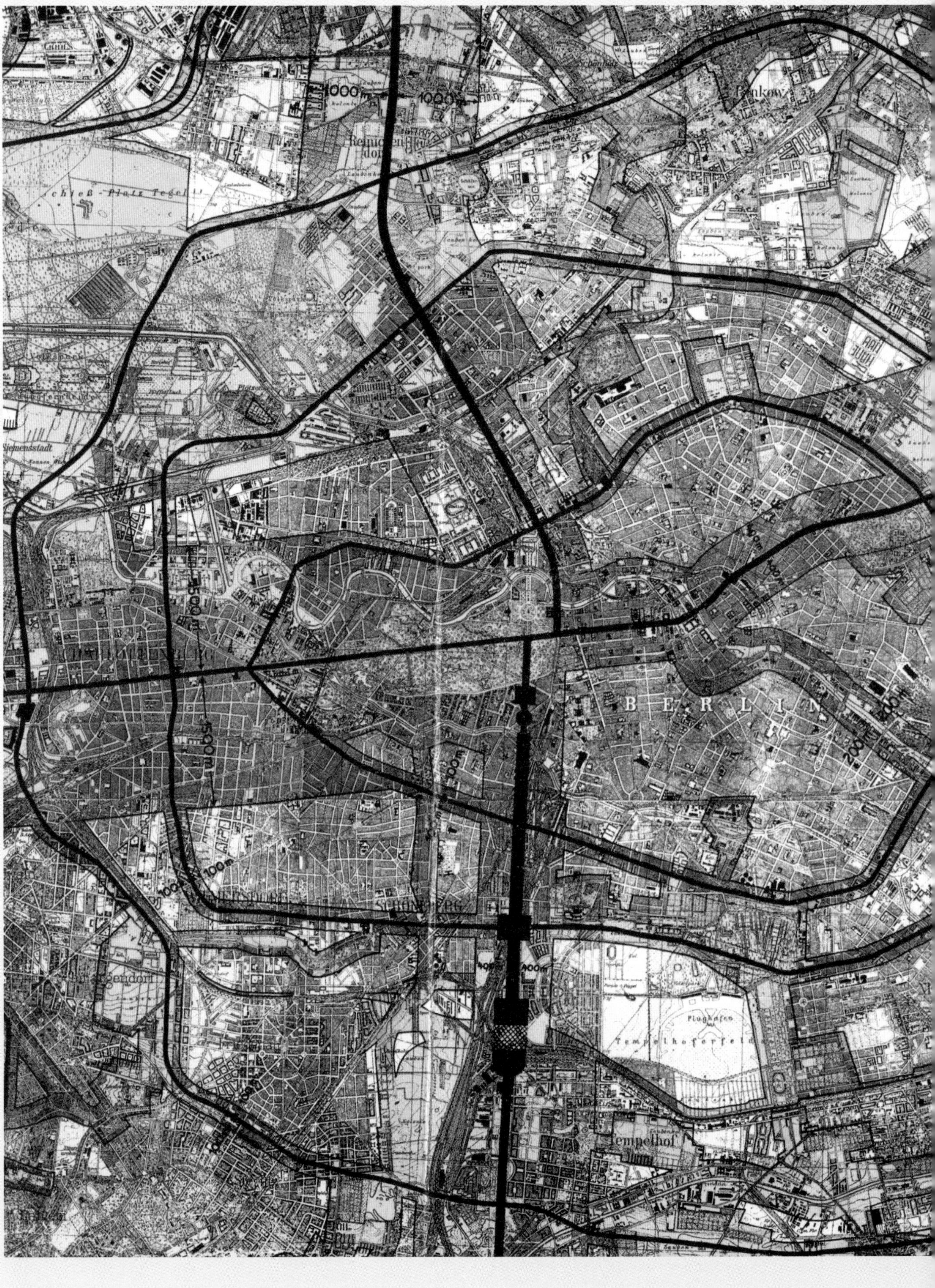
Pankow
Reinickendorf
Siemensstadt
B E R L I N
Tempelhof
Flughafen
Tempelhoferfeld
1000m
1500m
100m
400m
200m

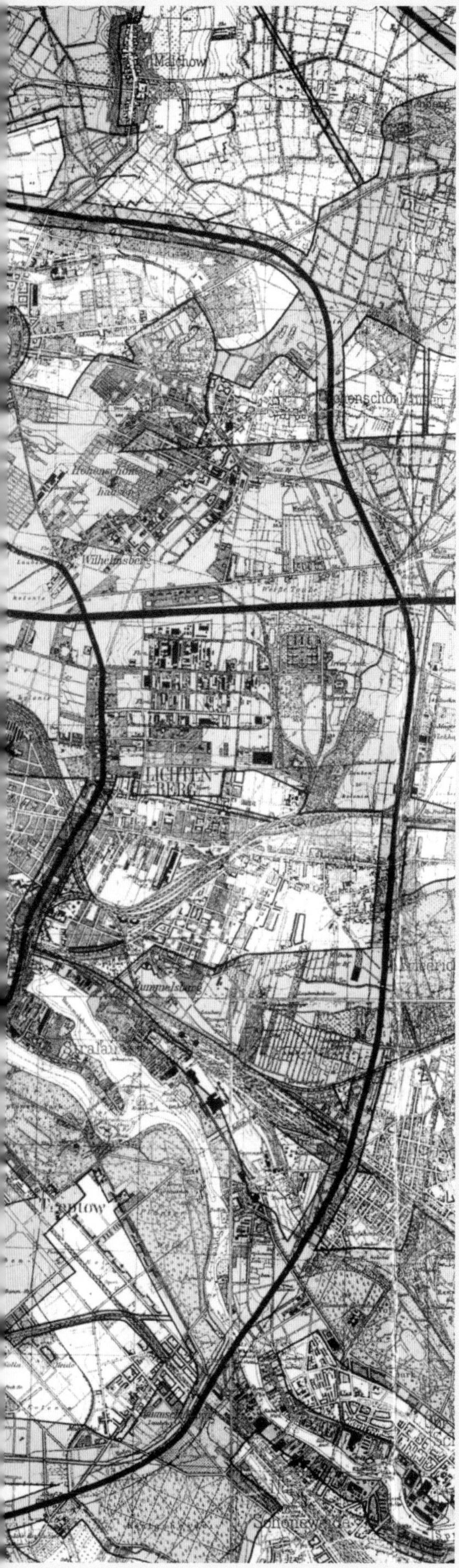
Malchow
LICHTEN
BERG

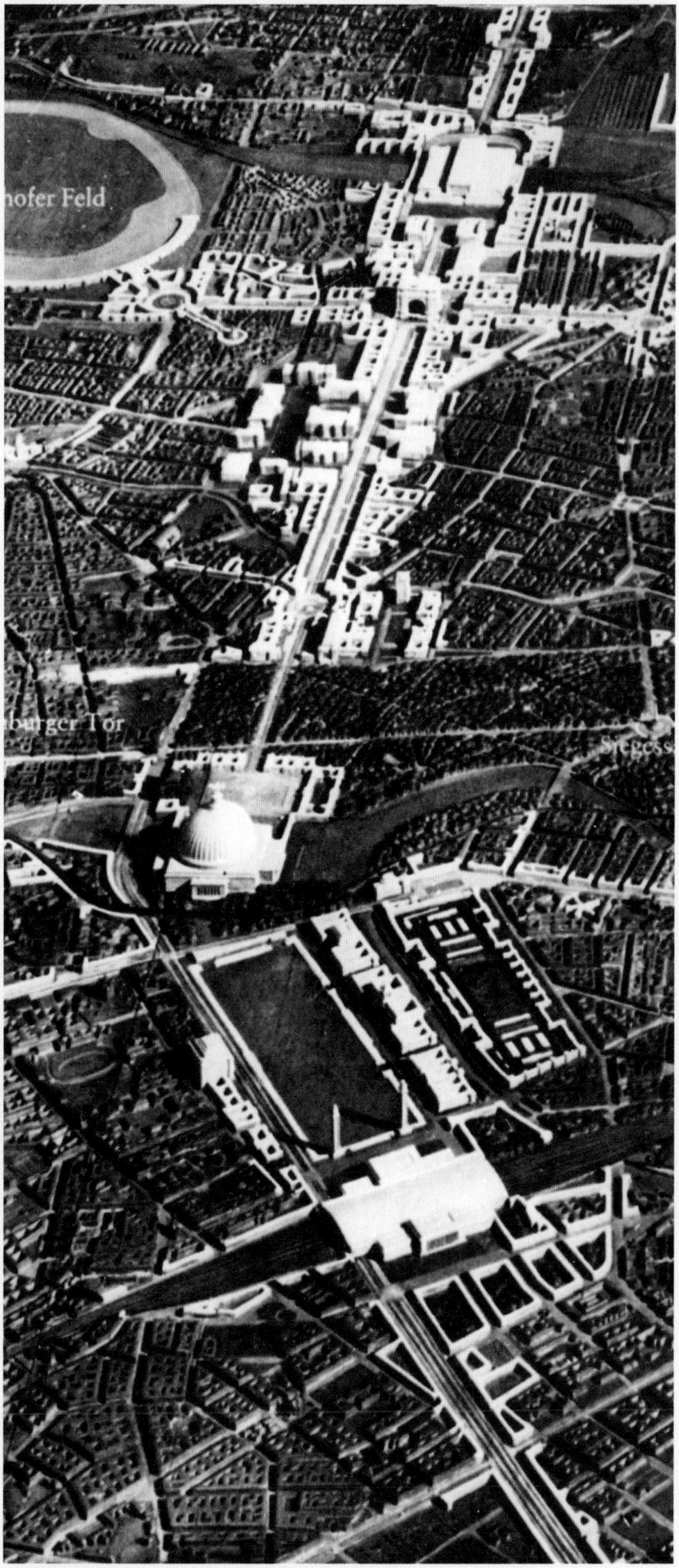
Feld
Tor

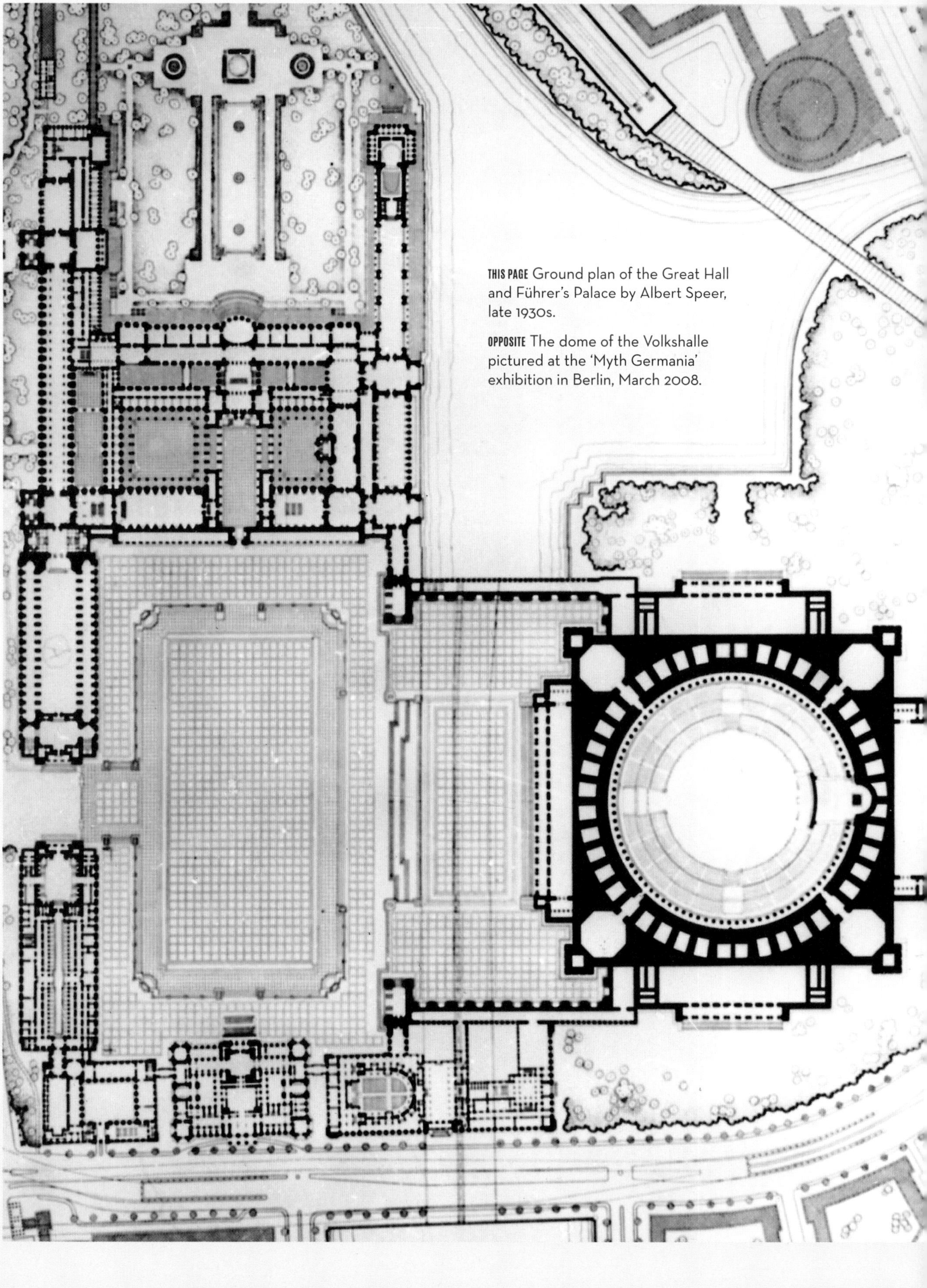

THIS PAGE Ground plan of the Great Hall and Führer's Palace by Albert Speer, late 1930s.

OPPOSITE The dome of the Volkshalle pictured at the 'Myth Germania' exhibition in Berlin, March 2008.

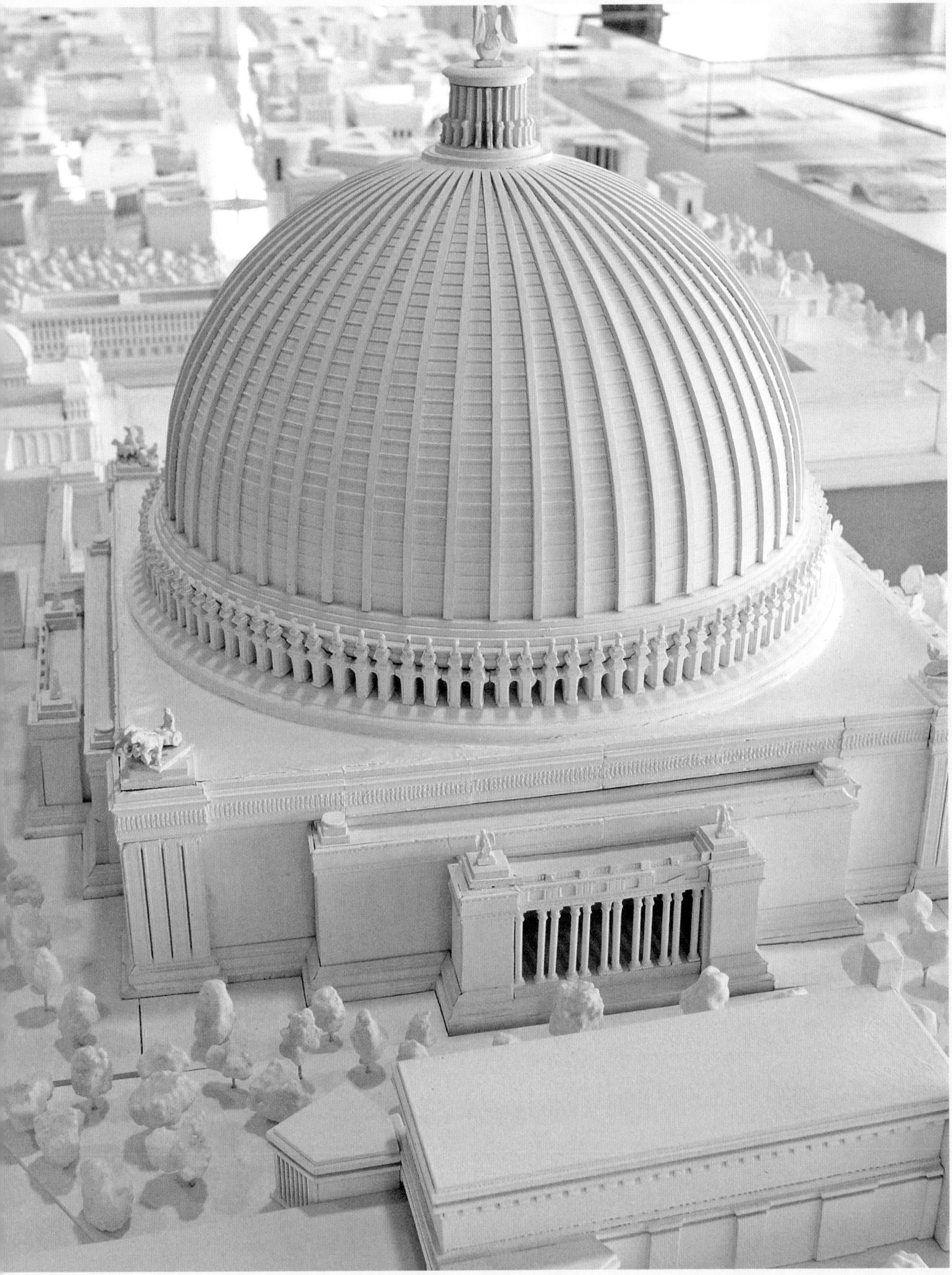

TOP Germania: Volkshalle miniature, designed by Albert Speer, late 1930s.

ABOVE Model of the layout of a road circus, Apollo-Brunnen, 1938.

OPPOSITE Plan of the Welthauptstadt Germania.

PRESTIGE

‘Build! Don’t Talk!’

MIES VAN DER ROHE

BERLIN'S POST-WAR REBUILDING

BERLIN, GERMANY 1950s-60s

When Berlin fell to the Red Army in 1945 it was a wasteland. There were so many blitzed buildings that the city's rubble – 100 million cubic yards of it – was enough for a manmade mountain called Teufelsberg, the Devil's Peak, on which the US National Security Agency built a huge listening station, the remains of which can still be broken into. Small wonder that Berlin became the tabula rasa on to which dreams were sketched by utopian architects and planners of the 1950s and 60s.

With the city divided, redevelopment became a competition between East and West. East Berlin's ambitious Alexanderplatz remodelling was completed at the end of the 60s, crowned by the priapic TV tower Berliners call the Telespargel: TV asparagus. West Berlin had big plans too. Responding to a 1957 planning competition for the city, British architects Alison and Peter Smithson imagined a West Berlin that would squat on multiple levels, connected by escalators. Alas, the Smithsons' scheme was never acted on.

Another of Berlin's post-war plans that bit the dust was perhaps the most bonkers idea of all: rolling pavements. This was the brainwave of Austrian architect Georg Kohlmaier and his Hungarian agency partner Barna von Sartory, the kind you might imagine after a long night watching sci-fi flicks and banging shots of schnapps. In German it sounds even better: *die Rollende Gehsteige am Kurfürstendamm*. They also proposed this system in Graz, Austria.

The issue was that Kurfürstendamm, the Oxford Street or Fifth Avenue of West Berlin, became clogged with traffic as car ownership began to rise in the 60s. The 1969 solution would be to put us two-legged problems (or people, as we're sometimes, but not often, called by urban planners) up above the motor melée.

But this wasn't just any old overhead walkway system. It was to be a giant steel snake, fat enough for double travelators, which would run the entire length of the Ku'damm. Each building would have direct access to the main 2km (1¼ mile) long tube via side-tubes that plugged directly into high-floor escape doors. The one existing drawing makes it look a bit like Carsten Höller's idea for office towers with slides emerging from upper levels, and, who knows, maybe Höller drew his inspiration from here?

Once inside the main tube, pedestrians – whose cars would be parked in a nearby multistorey – would be free to let their muscles further wither away by standing still while the travelator took them along the street, letting them sidestep into whichever shop or office they fancied via its tube. No daylight, no exertion, no budgetary care, no connection whatsoever to the reality of how we like to move around in cities – in short, the perfect 1960s urban plan that never happened. A feeling that the tubes were too ugly on the streetscape, combined with the cost, meant that the idea never got off the ground, so to speak.

The rolling pavements reared their fanciful head in 2015 at the Berlinische Galerie's excellent 'Radical Modern' exhibition, where they sat alongside other big architectural and planning dreams of mid-twentieth-century Berlin: from the aforementioned development of Alexanderplatz and the similarly themed Smithson plan (which also included multiple downtown heliports), to the never-achieved expansion of the now sadly shuttered Tegel Airport.

PREVIOUS PAGE Design for the Palace of the Soviets, Moscow.

OPPOSITE Plan for the post-war rebuilding of West Berlin.

5
6
4
1
2
3

AUSTIN
PHILIPS
KELSCH
KURIER

SEMPERIT
BÜCHER

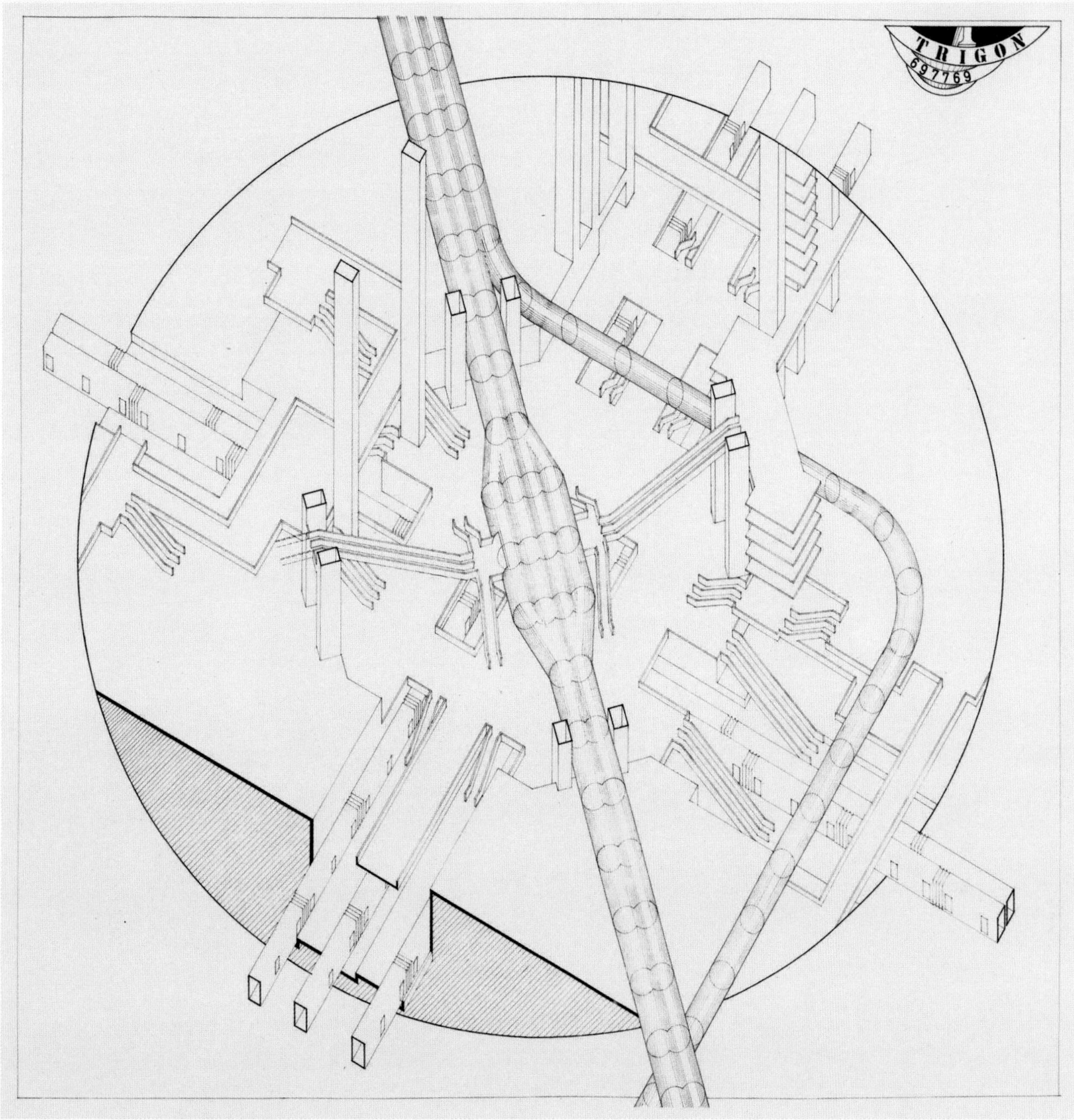

PREVIOUS PAGE Berlin's rolling pavements idea was also envisaged for Graz in this visualization.

OPPOSITE Rolling pavements passing through Breitscheidplatz, Berlin.

ABOVE A diagram of how rolling pavements could look in a city.

PLAN VOISIN

PARIS, FRANCE 1925

If, as some contend, architecture is really just a priapic parlour game, then Le Corbusier's Plan Voisin is the equivalent of short-man-in-a-sports-car syndrome.

Le Corbusier was a grouchy Swiss polymath who went on to dominate the design world in the 1950s and early 60s. But back in 1925 his plan to replace the buildings of central Paris with 18 identical skyscrapers was met with so much hostility that French commentators of the time had to put their cigarettes down to get their invective out. Le Corbusier's idea was to create a new future without resorting to the past. Yet Parisian *grands projets* have been with us since Haussmann straightened the city's crooked streets into grand boulevards in the late nineteenth century; and the big ideas didn't stop with Le Corbusier either.

While the Plan Voisin's drama and violence – knock down central Paris, remember – was immediately binned with yesterday's tattered *Le Figaro*, Le Corbusier's vision did actually inspire later projects. La Défense, Paris's proto-Canary Wharf business district on the west of the city, is a forest of skyscrapers that Le Corbusier would surely have approved of.

Developed from 1958 and still not really finished, this is the part of Paris that introduced a city previously unaccustomed to tall steel and glass buildings to the world of thrusting towers. They're not the same height or the same shape as the ones in the Plan Voisin, but the sentiment is the same.

In the 1960s, Paris's planners tinkered once more, and the results also recall the Plan Voisin. The sprawling outer-city housing estates that went up in *banlieues* such as Clichy-sous-Bois consisted of clusters of tower blocks that didn't look so different from Le Corbusier's ideas 40 years prior. While La Défense has prospered, these estates have fomented extremism and dislocation – not so much because

A series of towers rising in symmetrical patterns as part of Le Corbusier's Paris.

of the architecture *per se*, which is often modern, wild and extremely exciting, but due to the lack of public transport, jobs, social services and cultural amenities out in the suburbs.

Paris likes to keep its problems at arm's length. When Robert Hughes stopped by at a *banlieue* in 1979 when filming his bravura art-history epic for the BBC, *The Shock of the New*, his verdict on the – to him – terrible tower blocks he saw was damning: 'Gimmicky, condescending, Alphaville modernism.' *Alphaville* – Jean-Luc Godard's rich 1965 noir film – predicted a Paris of some time over the horizon taken over by towers which demeaned the citizen. It made Parisians freak out about the future. Yet Le Corbusier's original Plan Voisin didn't contain any of this muck and grit.

Was he optimistic or stupid? His original drawings depict swathes of green space between buildings, aeroplanes gliding around, people taking tea on terraces. He didn't want to unleash a demon, but he ended up doing just that.

OPPOSITE Plan Voisin was as much a provocation as a vision – Le Corbusier's radical intent was shocking.

BELOW The Plan Voisin envisaged razing parts of Paris and replacing the historic buildings with skyscrapers.

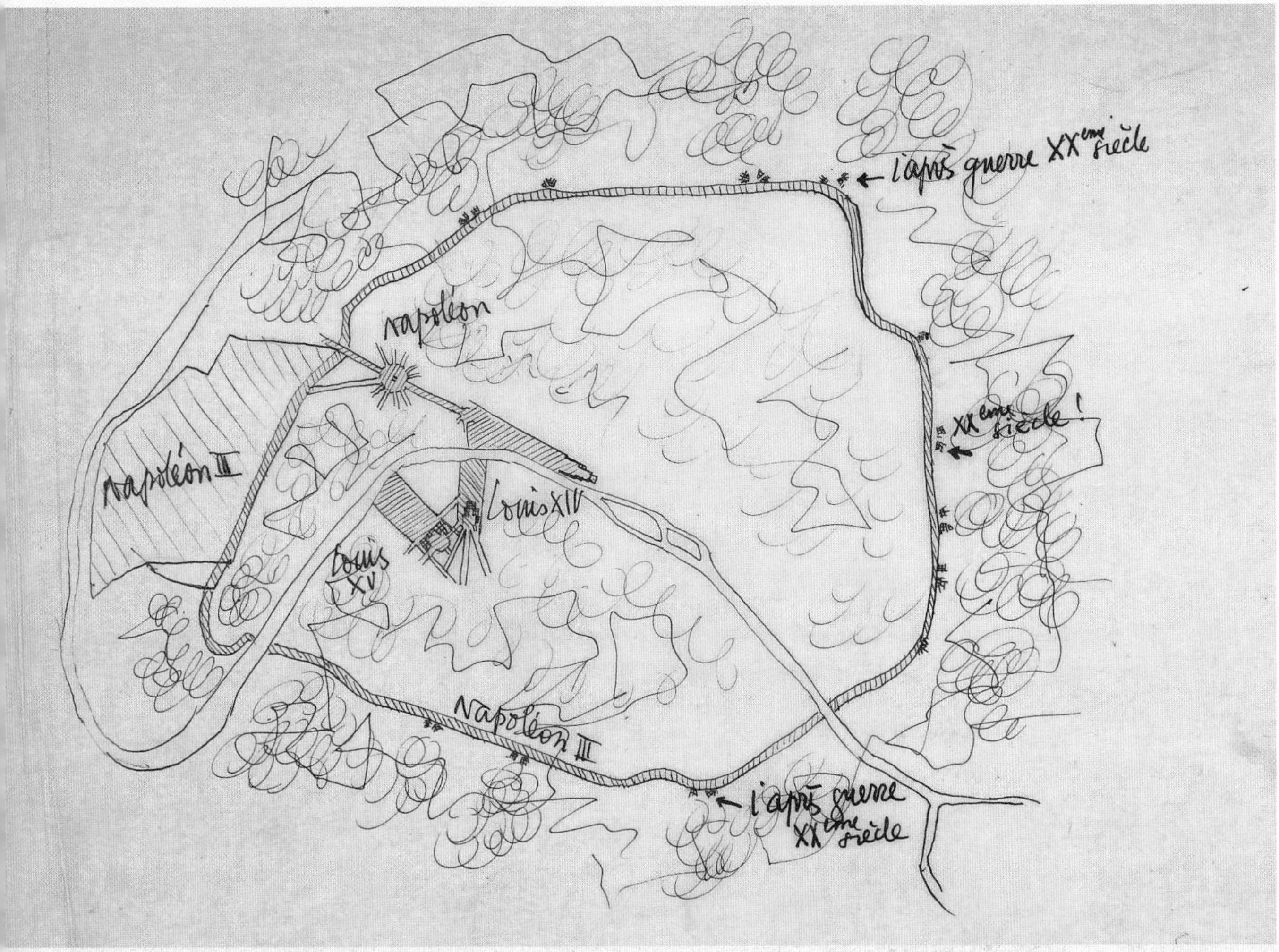
l'après guerre XXème siècle
napoléon
Napoléon III
Louis XIV
Louis XV
XXème siècle!
Napoléon III
l'après guerre XXème siècle

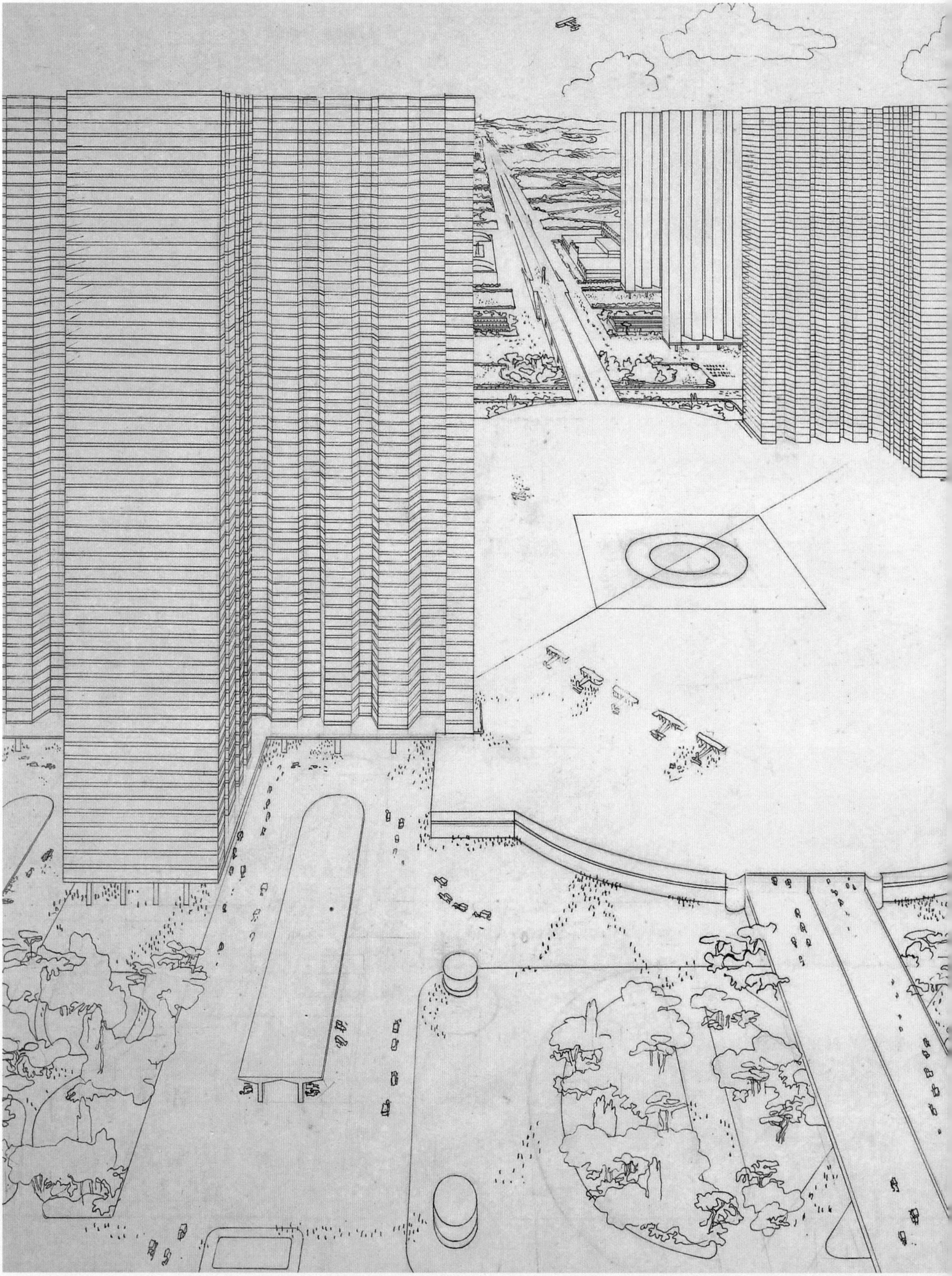

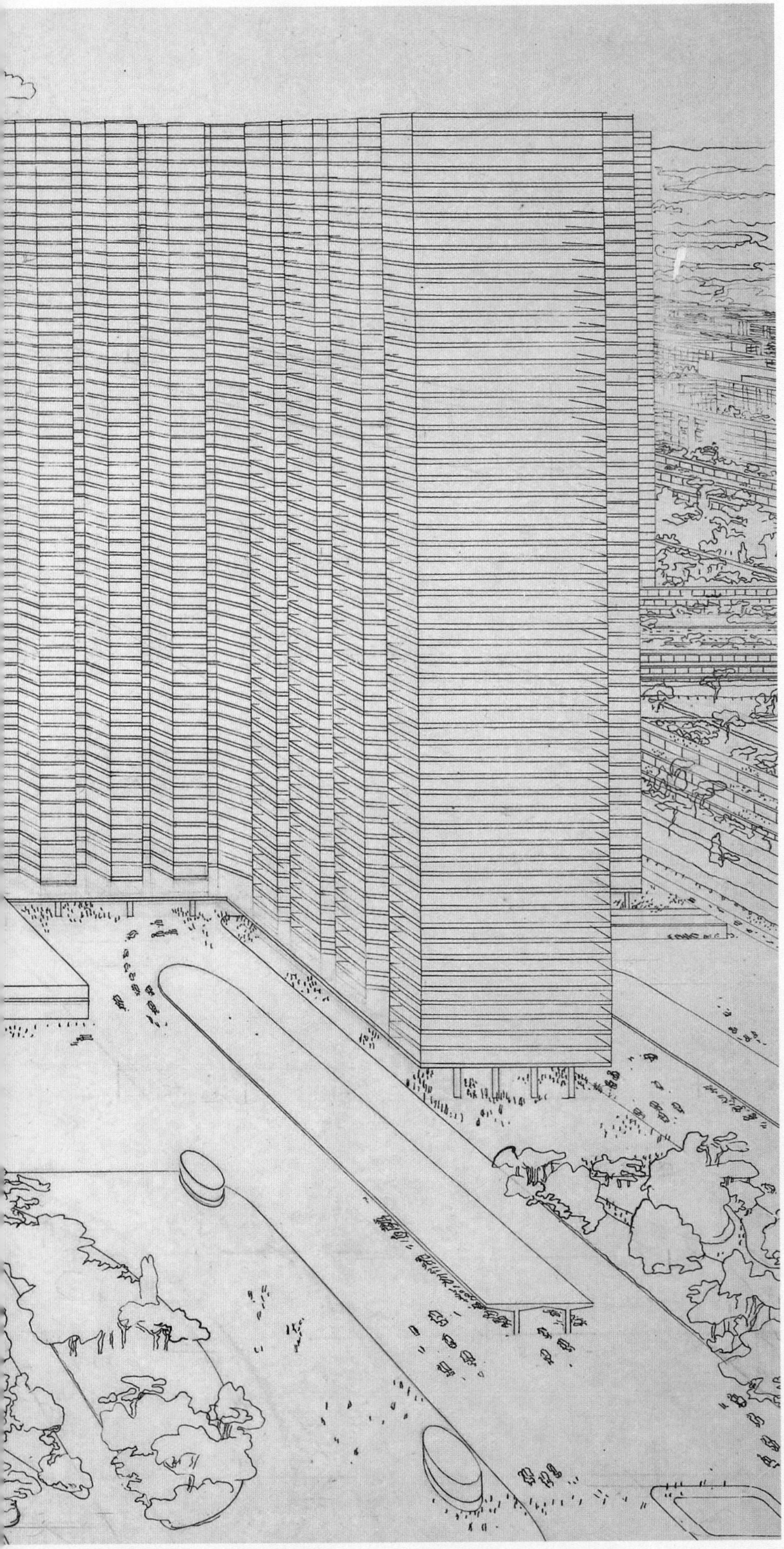

The proposed towers of the Plan Voisin rising over Paris.

PALACE OF THE SOVIETS

MOSCOW, USSR 1930s

Having a professional interest in the most significant outdoor pools in the world, my attention was grabbed by the Moskva Pool, which only existed from 1960 to 1994, when I was writing my book *Lido*. In the end it didn't make the cut, as the book focused on extant pools you could actually dive into. The story of what was one of the world's largest outdoor pools links that book with this one, because that pool was supposed to be something very different – it was essentially the filled-in foundations of the legendary and legendarily cancelled Palace of the Soviets. A tale which shows that even once construction has started, it doesn't mean a project will necessarily be finished (Sagrada Familia, anyone?).

The 1931 competition – part of a wider plan to modernize Moscow – was organized as a ruse by Stalin to cement his power; 160 entries came in, from Walter Gropius and our old friend Le Corbusier, and Russians like Moisei Ginzburg and Vladimir Shchuko. As is often the case when politicians are involved, there was much meddling. A design was eventually settled on which tied together Shchuko's designs with those by Vladimir Gelfreikh and Boris Iofan. This neo-classical wedding cake would be topped with the marzipan figure that no bride would have ordered from the bakers – a 100-metre-high Lenin, making it the tallest building in the world. The Second World War then intervened, and despite the steel frame having been sunk, it was cut out again and used for military purposes – an indication of how desperate the USSR must have been with the Wehrmacht at the gates of the city.

Surprisingly, the Palace of the Soviets wasn't constructed after the Soviet victory against Germany. Instead the site of the former Cathedral of Christ the Saviour (blown up for the Palace project) was eventually opened as the huge swimming pool. When that pool itself closed down, and communism did too, a copy of the cathedral was raised on its original site and the Palace story became just another Moscow memory – as with plans for a House of Books, House of Technology, an elaborate Belarus Station, and El Lissitzky's far more modern and impressive Cloud Iron skyscrapers – none of which were realized either.

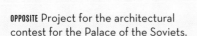

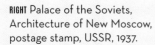

OPPOSITE Project for the architectural contest for the Palace of the Soviets.

RIGHT Palace of the Soviets, Architecture of New Moscow, postage stamp, USSR, 1937.

ABOVE Design for the Palace of the Soviets by architect Boris Iofan.

ABOVE A model of the Palace of the Soviets and its environs by Boris Iofan, 1934.

The Palace of the Soviets, depicted in 1944.

TOKYO BAY PLAN

TOKYO, JAPAN 1960

Today, when we think of an Asian powerhouse, it's China. Not so long ago though, it was Japan. In recent years it has been seen as the paradigm case of a nation coping with economic stagnation. But from the 1950s to well into the 1970s, the country was light years ahead of its competition: defeated in war, like Germany, yet it too was booming.

And no single architect did as much to shape the style, look and ethos of Japan's urban fabric during that heady period as Kenzō Tange. Like J.G. Ballard, Tange spent some of his childhood in Shanghai. But where Ballard saw man's inhumanity, the dystopias we accidentally create, the mess and gore and violence we seem sometimes to revel in, Tange saw the capacity for technology and a benevolent kind of progress with which to build fantastical new cities straight from the pages of comic books.

He used tropes from Japan's past to ameliorate the radicalism of his designs – joints that you see in temples, that kind of thing. But he really ripped up the rule book otherwise. His Yoyogi National Gym for the Tokyo 1964 Olympics was a structural triumph: a suspension bridge designed as a gym, a roof supported like a road would be over a river. Working in raw concrete, his madly abstracted buildings like the Yamanashi Press and Broadcasting Centre became emblems of the brutalist movement – complete flights of fancy.

But Tange was rigorous and his ideas came from deep thought and scientific study. He'd also worked up a plan for Boston Harbour. With his 1960 Tokyo Bay Plan he envisaged Tokyo expanding into its bay. From prêt-à-porter to pâtisserie, Tokyo is obsessed with Paris, and there's something very French, very Haussmannian about the grand axis Tange wanted to feed across the bay: like a Champs-Élysées surrounded by water. Each side of the axis (comprising freeways and services) would be platforms like oil rigs, on which would sit crazy combinations of buildings, stacked up and plugged in to each other. The project sank, eventually – but its legacy never went away, especially down the coast in Osaka.

When Osaka was building its new airport 30 years later it created an artificial island and strung a straight causeway out to it. All very Tange. And 10 years after the Tokyo Bay Plan, Japan's biggest moment in the architectural spotlight was the Expo at Osaka 1970, the event at which many commentators like Douglas Murphy contend modernism died. This was the last time we dreamed big. And the plan for Osaka '70? It was by Tange, of course. The megastructures and the grand axes were lifted straight from his earlier Tokyo Bay Plan.

Tange worked well into his eighties and produced edifices like the huge Tokyo City Government Building. But it's for his capsules and his plug-in buildings, his megastructures and his unbuilt ideas, that he'll always be known. He catapulted Japan into the future. But he could have taken it even further.

WILL ALSOP IN YORKSHIRE

BRADFORD AND BARNSLEY, UK 2003

Chain-smoking *bon viveur* Will Alsop brought freshness and fun to a British architectural world that began to get some self-confidence back in the 1990s. The new millennium offered an opportunity for celebration and many cultural buildings were commissioned in the UK – many flopped harder than a drunk dad diving into a Benidorm swimming pool, but that's a story for another day. Alsop offered bold visions for industrial towns, the likes of which hadn't been seen for half a century. His plans came with colour and cheek – he wanted to remodel coal town Barnsley in 2003 after the Tuscan splendour of Lucca, with tech-age twists. And for my own home town, Bradford, he imagined turning a city centre that was rich with Victorian edifices but suffering from severe economic malaise into something spectacular – with a centrepiece lake surrounded by wonky postmodern fun palaces. Several years later he was up to similar tricks in an unrealized plan for Croydon.

An Alsop building – Peckham Library in particular – makes one smile, and it would have been of huge interest to see his playful proposals (he also had similar thoughts about other problematic English towns like Middlesbrough, Stoke-on-Trent and Walsall) come to life on a larger canvas.

OMA'S VERTICAL CITIES

BANGKOK, MUMBAI, DUBAI, TUNIS 1996-2008

Rem Koolhaas's Dutch studio continued to fly the flag for large-scale, avant-garde architecture as modernism was retreating and the meek and the twee were sneaking back into the mainstream milieu. To wit: Rotterdam's Office for Metropolitan Architecture's 1996 proposal for the kilometre-high Hyperbuilding in Bangkok would have housed 120,000 and contained a variety of high-tech transport options like cable cars and high-speed elevators and funiculars. Their 2006 proposal for the Dubai Renaissance was a standard 300m high slab block ... ah, but with a comical twist – the entire skyscraper would be constantly rotating. Stay at a friend's if hungover. Looking like a giant model of two synapses, the 2008 India Tower in Mumbai would have included a hotel and housing with a viewing platform at the point where the two volumes met. The same year they came up with a double-skyscraper proposal for Tunis – The Twins, which would also be a mixed-use beast.

None of these were built. But OMA did go on to build much – notably the CCTV Headquarters in Beijing and Seattle's Central Library.

Design for The Twins, Tunis.

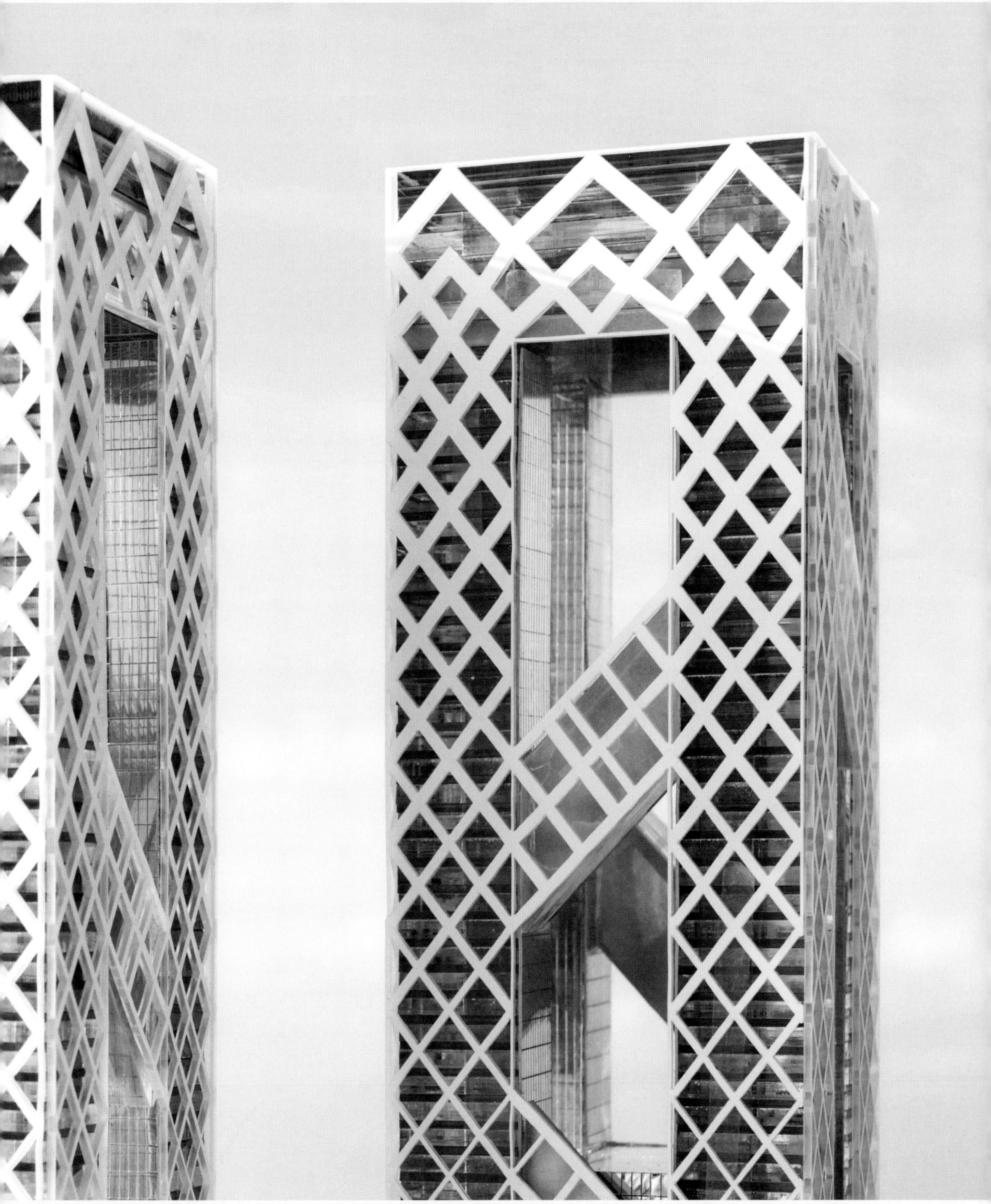

BELOW Design for Hyperbuilding, Bangkok.

BELOW Design for the rotating Renaissance Dubai.

OVERLEAF Skyline featuring the Renaissance Dubai.

Maybank

LOUIS KAHN IN PHILADELPHIA

PHILADEPHIA, USA 1950s-60s

Louis Kahn's home city of Philadelphia came under his microscope as he sought to remodel it for the twentieth century. A 1952 idea of keeping traffic running round the outside of the central business district and parking cars in spiral garages on the periphery was said by Peter Reed to have been inspired by Kahn's interest in Carcassonne's famous city walls, which captivated him on a visit.

Also around this time he came up with a pioneering idea for a skyscraper, the City Tower, of an asymmetric shape, predating the kind of deconstructivist designs we'd see much later. Kahn wanted to design a new home for the Philadelphia College of Art and also several synagogues. In the end none of these projects saw the light of day. In fact, Kahn designed many buildings that would never appear, even in places as exotic as Luanda and Tehran, as his fame spread globally.

The Triangle Area Redevelopment plan for Philadelphia.

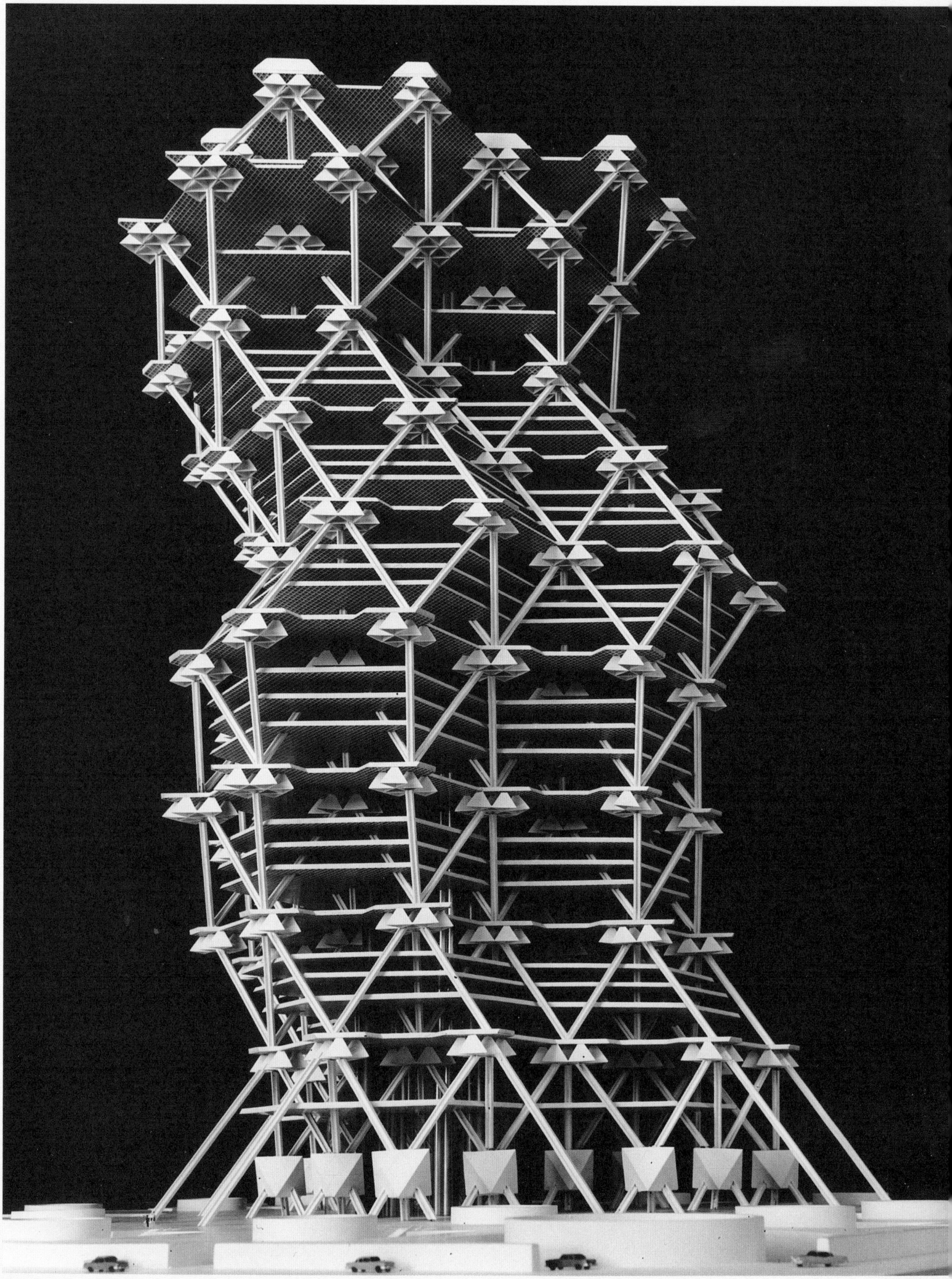

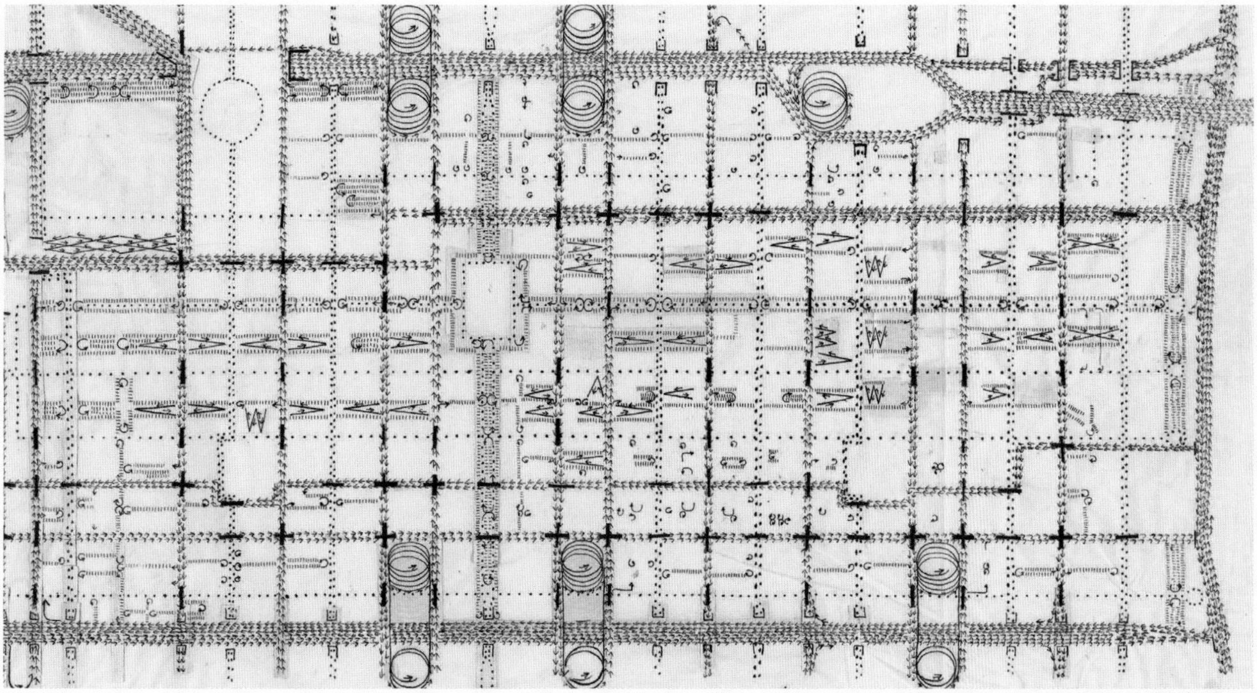

TOP Plan for the Civic Center in Philadelphia.

ABOVE Kahn's traffic study for his Philadelphia plan.

OPPOSITE Plan for a high-rise tower in Philadelphia.

THREE SAN FRANCISCO PLANS

SAN FRANCISCO, USA 1905/1942/1969

San Francisco is notable for its opposition to grand plans, which fomented at the end of the 1950s and crystallized a decade later when the 1968 hippies hung out at Haight-Ashbury and thinkers on the same wavelength spread their leftfield ideas around the world, questioning the fundamentals of authority and capitalism. Right around this time, incredibly perhaps, the firm of Wurster, Bernardi & Emmons proposed a high-density infilling of the Lands End district, covering up the old Sutro Baths with a slab block and some lower-rise brutalist buildings not too distant in style from John Portman's Hyatt Regency, which opened over on the Embarcadero in 1973. This was next to where the infamous freeway that partially collapsed in the 1989 earthquake was later torn down (freeway revolts had become extremely common in San Francisco).

Earlier, an even more bizarre plan was put forward by John Reber, a theatre producer who believed that damming San Francisco Bay would have been a good idea. He wanted to create a freshwater lake for potable purposes and additionally build an airport, port and military facilities, and freeways on top of the dams. The ambitious – some might say hare-brained – Reber Plan gained some traction through the 1940s, receiving Congressional money for a feasibility study, yet it was never acted on.

An even earlier attempt at rationalism was Daniel Burnham's 1905 shot at masterplanning San Francisco. He envisaged a kind of hybrid garden city featuring the boulevards and blocks of Barcelona's modernisme expansion melting into the parks and neo-classicism of Washington D.C.

OPPOSITE The Reber Plan for San Francisco Bay, 1942.

BELOW Bird's eye view of the Burnham Plan for San Francisco, 1905.

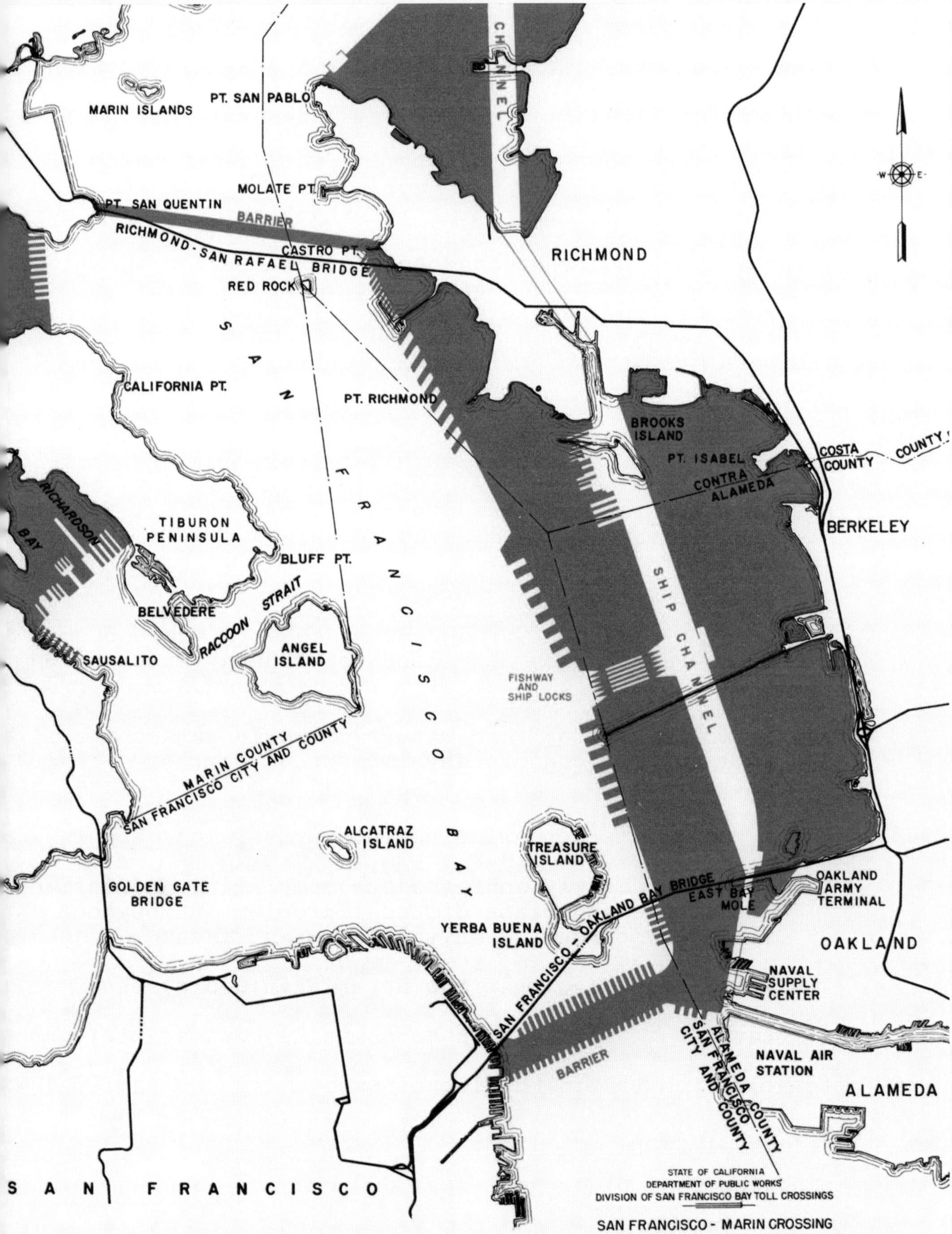

PROPOSED BARRIERS IN SAN FRANCISCO BAY

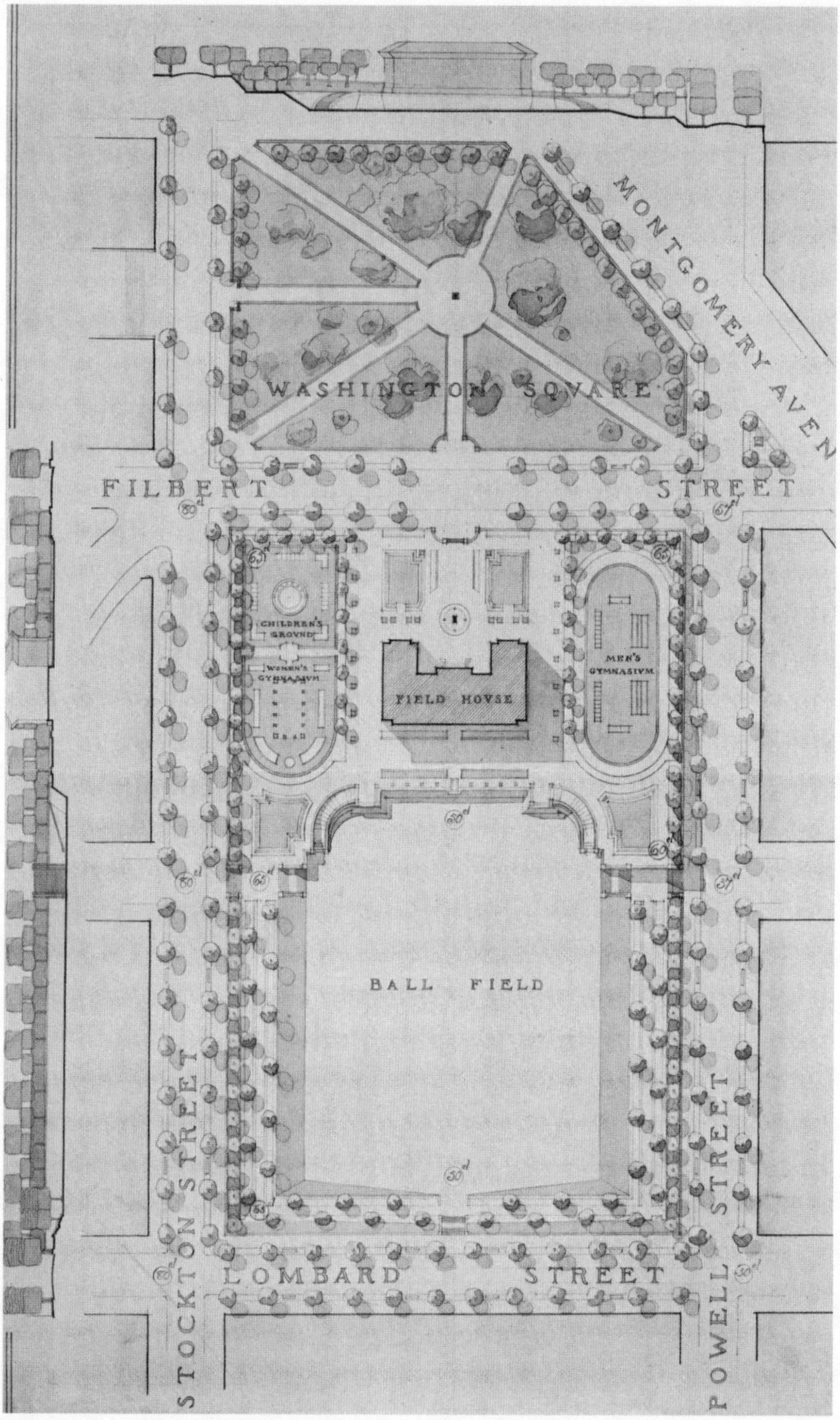

ABOVE Washington Square Plan, part of the 1905 Burnham Plan.

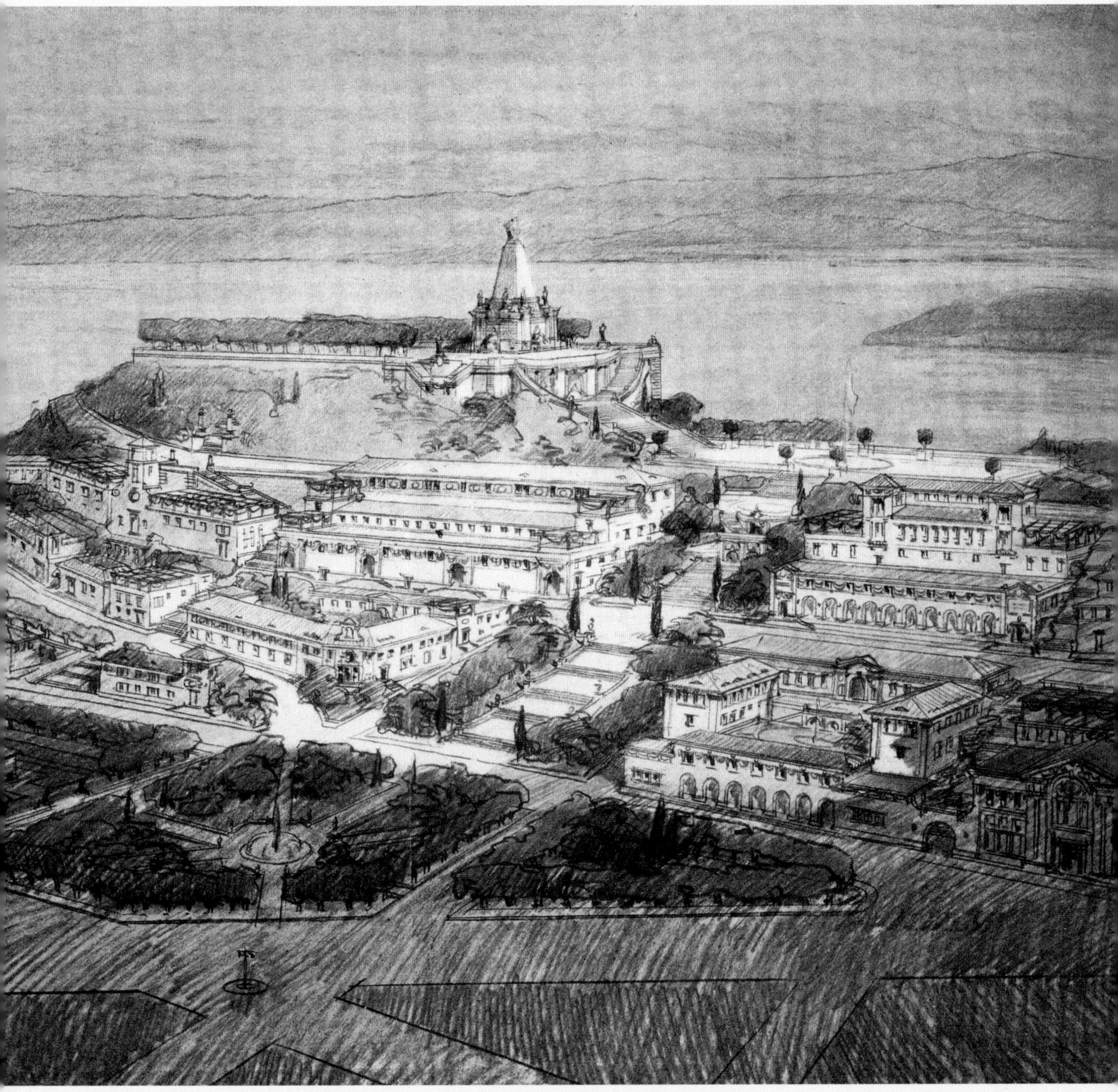

ABOVE Telegraph Hill proposals, Burnham Plan, 1905.

OVERSIZED ART AND MAD MONUMENTS

When does art become architecture? It's a moot point – does a large artwork need to have a function other than decoration? There's certainly been no shortage of artists with a megalomaniacal disposition who've been keen as mustard to throw up works which have a bad case of elephantiasis. Sometimes, if we call them 'monuments' and give them a purpose, they make more sense to the man in the street and the tabloid hack and are thus easier to push through the planning stages. Still, it didn't help in getting many monuments actually constructed.

Millard Sheets' 'Monument to Democracy' (1954) has something of the Rockefeller Center about it; figures holding up a giant globe were to be 150 metres high and perched on the California seafront at San Pedro.

Daniel Chester French and Thomas Hastings came up with a scheme for a 'National American Indian Monument' (1913) comprising a 50-metre high warrior to sit at Fort Tompkins on Staten Island, New York.

In Washington D.C. in the early 1920s the 'Mother's Monument' was to be a tribute to those who fell in the defence of the United States. A 30-metre-high art deco behemoth would have sat on top of rising ground to grandiose effect.

There's a plan currently tabled to build a Colossus of Rhodes straddling the harbour entrance in Rhodes, Greece. The proposals have been around since 2008 and call for a 150-metre man with a light in his head and steps up the inside of his leg. The dimensions of his potentially colossal manhood have yet to be revealed.

In London in 1904 there were serious plans to build a huge monumental tower next to the Houses of Parliament. The massive 170-metre 'Imperial Monumental Tower' would have made Big Ben seem pokey by comparison. The house style was neo-gothic (no surprise) and the architects were Edward Buckton Lamb and John Pollard Seddon. A hall would have displayed booty nabbed from around the world ... sorry 'treasures of the Empire'.

In the wake of Manhattan's High Line, monstrous copies have been dealt out like bad hands at a craps table. The worst of the lot was London's Garden Bridge from Thomas Heatherwick in 2013, which was furiously opposed by almost everyone and prompted really quite high levels of ire, leading to its cancellation.

Australia is home to all sorts of tongue-in-cheek big things – the Big Prawn and the Big Banana being some of the more famous – but in 2019 the Central Coast staked a plan to build a Big Pelican, as it's home to many of the exotic birds. While not quite art, what they are exactly is not immediately clear.

Perhaps the weirdest and most compelling of these supersized animal artworks, though, was Mark Wallinger's planned 2009 lifelike horse – a 50-metre-high white stallion, which would have sat on the pancake-flat marshes at Ebbsfleet in Kent – immediately recognizable to Eurostar passengers from France and Belgium who pass the spot in their thousands each day.

The largest and most spectacular works of modern times evoke the spirit of the Nazca Lines or Avebury Stone Circle. The great American land art projects seemed to reflect on a moment in time before ecological collapse, when humans thought themselves once more masters of the universe, when the huge post-war building boom reshaped the whole world. Michael Heizer's 'City' in the Nevada Desert, for example, was begun in the early 1970s but is due to be finally finished soon.

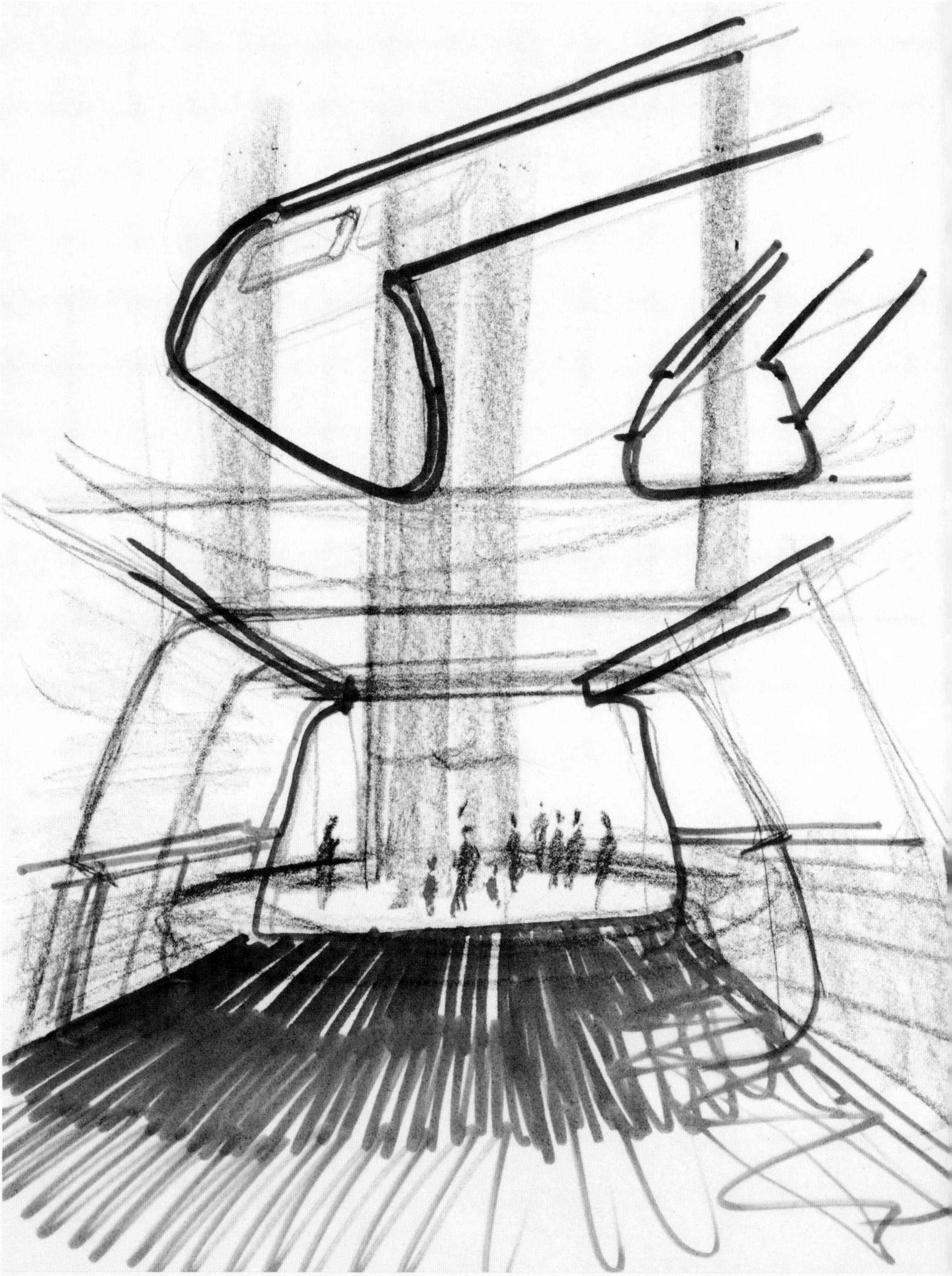

CULTURE

'I remember visiting Berlin in 1995 to see Christo's Reichstag wrapping ... that's when it became clear to me that people are very interested in fantastic projects – those projects that make fantasy become reality.'

ZAHA HADID, INTERVIEW WITH THE AUTHOR

SINGAPORE CLOUD

SINGAPORE 1989

Geoffrey Bawa's tropical modernism popped up in his native Sri Lanka, throughout India, in Mauritius, the Maldives and Indonesia. When his career was at a mature stage in the late 1980s the next plan was for a cloud forest under a huge glass pyramid at Singapore's Botanical Gardens. There were to be three smaller glass pyramids arrayed around one giant one, with the final plans tabled in 1989 – the same year that I.M. Pei's controversial glass pyramid was erected outside the Louvre in Paris.

PREVIOUS PAGE Sketch of a junction in Cedric Price's Fun Palace for Joan Littlewood.

BELOW Elevation drawing of Bawa's Cloud Forest Biosphere.

Singapore eventually got its cloud forest when the new Gardens by the Bay, opened in 2011, later built a kind of giant beetle-shaped glasshouse, with shades of Santiago Calatrava in its design, full of tropical plants. Changi Airport's Jewel, from 2019, is another elaborate enclosed garden with a huge waterfall. Bawa's most famous completed work, meanwhile, is probably the Parliament of Sri Lanka.

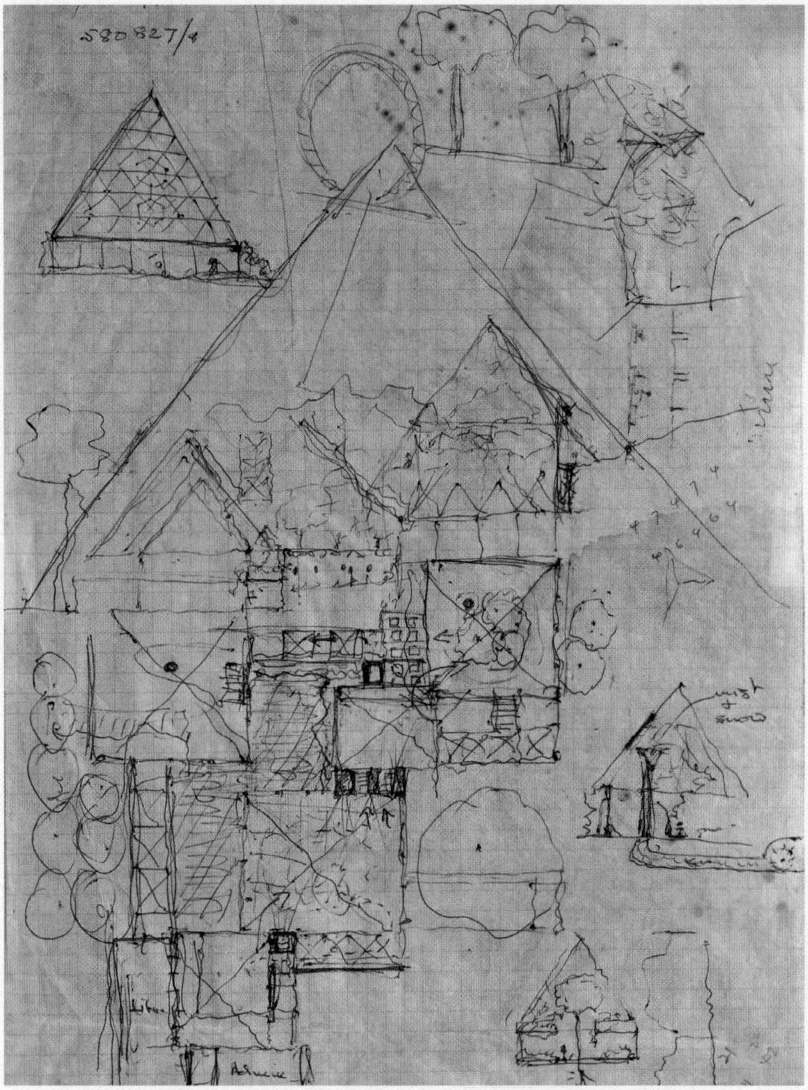

LEFT Sketch of the Cloud Centre by Geoffrey Bawa.

BELOW A cross-section through the main area of the botanical display.

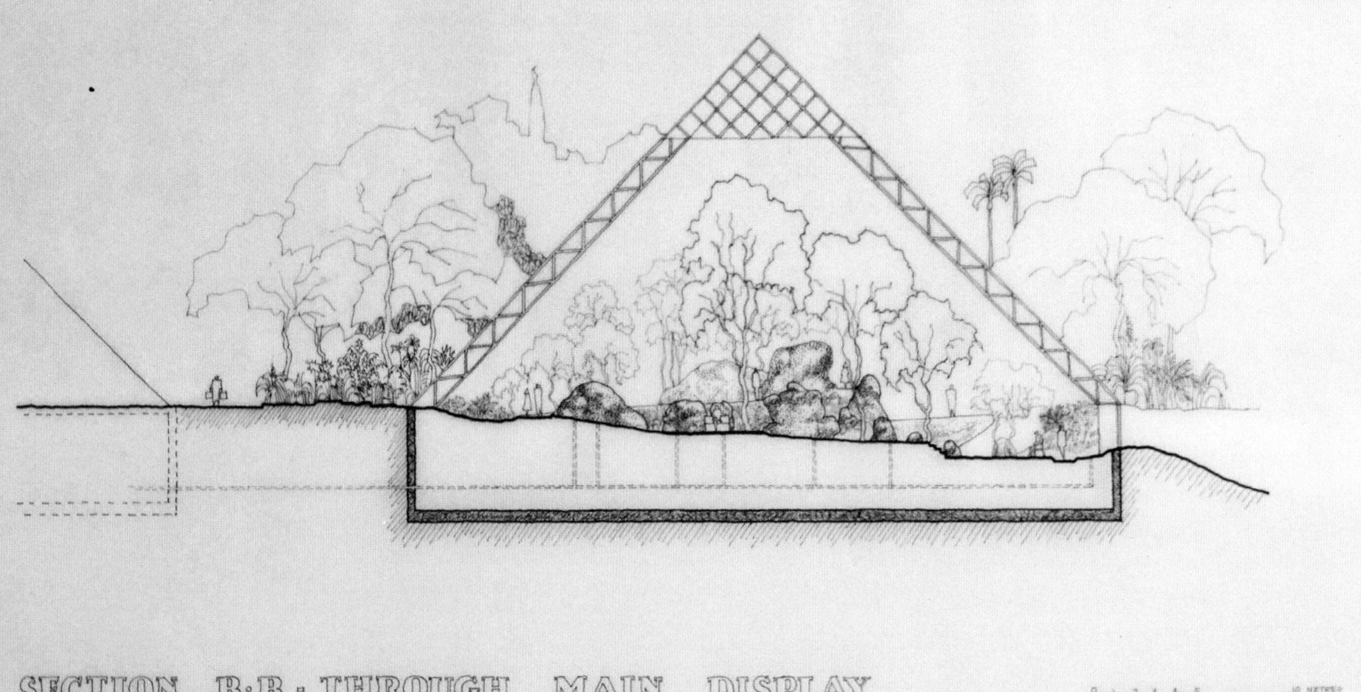

MODERN ART MUSEUM

CARACAS, VENEZUELA 1954

A site in Colinas de Bello Monte, a plush suburb of Caracas, was identified for the construction of a new art museum in 1954, and a year later Brazil's architecture playboy Oscar Niemeyer came up with a plan for it. Caracas back then was a different beast, before Venezuela's sad and lengthy decline. This clifftop site, near the now-emptied US Embassy, would have seen an inverted trapezoid teetering on a ledge overlooking the city. Inside: four floors of galleries and rooftop sculpture terrace. The whole thing would have been self-supporting.

There are memories of this building in two later Niemeyer works: the Chamber of Deputies at the Palace of Congress in Brasilia from 1960 and a very similar idea for the Niterói Contemporary Art Museum in Rio de Janeiro in 1996. But both of these were true 'bowl' shapes, not the trapezoid proposed for Caracas – unsurprising, as Niemeyer was fond of curves on buildings and, famously, women.

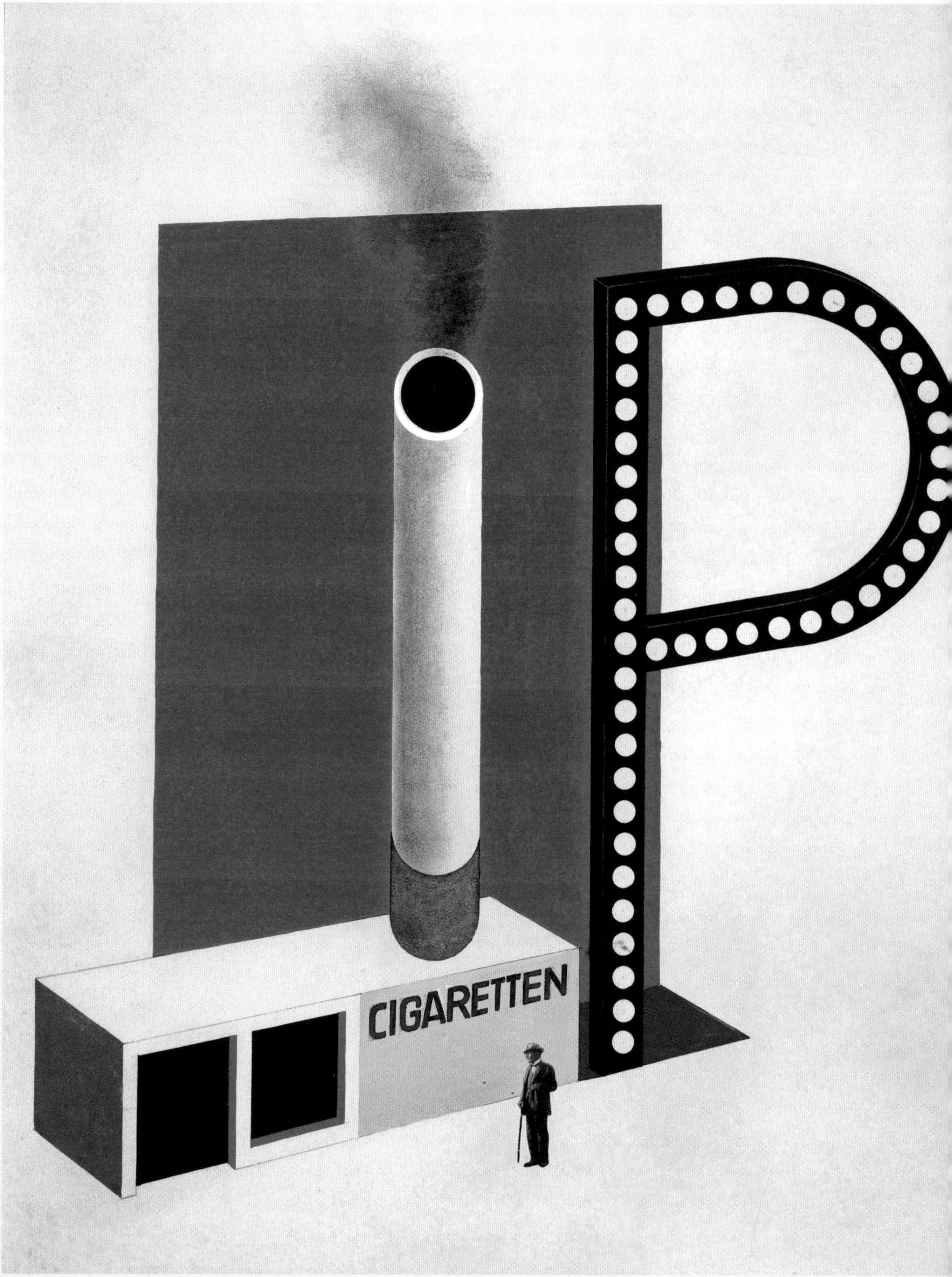
CIGARETTEN

HERBERT BAYER'S BAUHAUS KIOSKS

DESSAU, GERMANY 1924

If you had to choose one thing that wasn't built but you wish it was, why not Herbert Bayer's glorious series of 'small architecture'? The problem of the street has never really been solved successfully despite our many attempts – but here are prototypes that are enchanting and ready to be rolled out *en masse*; they look dazzling and fresh even almost a century after Bayer, an Austrian graphic designer who trained under Kandinsky at the Bauhaus, dreamt them up.

The primacy of type itself on the buildings aids immediate recognition, likewise the almost postmodern tactic of making something look like the something it sells – note the hilariously huge cartoon-like puffing cigarette on the tobacconist's stand. The colours owe a debt perhaps to Mondrian and the presentation of the project evokes Schwitters' collages. As well as the kiosks flogging fags and mags, Bayer formulated a plan for a cinema and a retail store.

Please can someone build these? Thanks.

OPPOSITE Bayer's idea for a cigarette stand.

BELOW Bayer's design for a cinema.

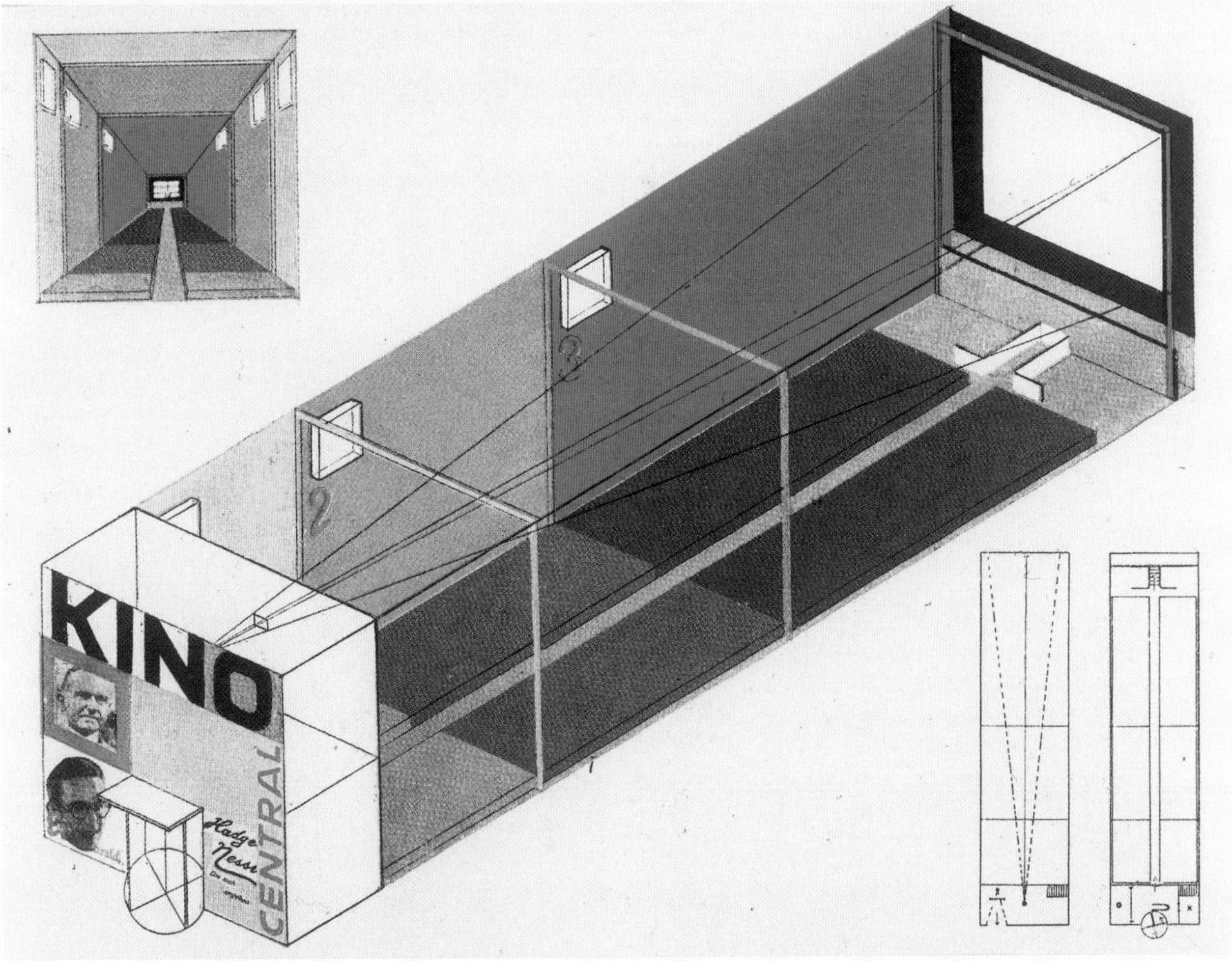

WHAT MIGHT HAVE BECOME OF SYDNEY OPERA HOUSE

SYDNEY, AUSTRALIA 1957

Sydney Opera House's gestation could be filed under 'problematic', if we're going to label it in a politely Anglo-Saxon way. Sydneysiders would no doubt have rather coarser words to describe the whole drawn-out process. In the end Jorn Utzon's Opera House opened years behind schedule in 1973, yet despite him leaving the job halfway through it became regarded as a masterpiece and the rest was history.

However, the story could have been very different. The 1955–57 design competition included entries from around the world and some of the shortlisted losers included Paul Boissevain and Barbara Osmond's double boxes, and Leon Loschetter, George Qualls, Walter Weisman and Robert Geddes's circular drum design. Vine & Vine meanwhile proposed a jaunty kind of South Bank/Scandi modernism of the 1950s à la National Theatre. None of these other proposals could hold a candle to Utzon's ideas and for once the correct decision was made. Nevertheless, the ineptitude of the politicians involved in the project almost put the Opera House itself in our unbuilt list: Utzon was pushed out, the whole thing nearly petered out, and the end result was also, sadly, slightly watered down.

OPPOSITE, ABOVE The D.R. Pritchard design: one of the finalists on display at the Art Gallery of New South Wales, January 1957.

OPPOSITE, BELOW The Philadelphia Collaborative Group plan for the Sydney Opera House, 31 January 1957. The design won second place in the overall competition.

ABOVE Paul Boissevain and Barbara Osmond's design, which won third place in the international competition, 30 January 1957.

LATE EDITION

FORECASTS (for 24 hours from 6 a.m.): CITY: Fine. Very warm. Fresh NE winds. N.S.W.: Fine mostly. Patchy rain, thunder on northern inland. Becoming hot in west and south with very high or extreme fire danger.

The Sydney Morning Herald.

PRICE, 4d

SUN: To-day, rises 5.14, sets 7.02. MOON: Rises 4.29 a.m., sets 6.19 p.m. TIDES (Fort Denison): High, 8.00 a.m. (5ft 4in), 8.28 p.m. (4ft 1in). Low, 1.35 a.m. (1ft 2in), 2.33 p.m. (10in).

No. 37,165 TELEPHONE: B0944 ONE HUNDRED AND TWENTY-SIXTH YEAR OF PUBLICATION 30 PAGES SYDNEY, WEDNESDAY, JANUARY 30, 1957

● Joern Utzon's winning design for a National Opera House at Benelong Point.

DANE'S CONTROVERSIAL DESIGN WINS OPERA HOUSE CONTEST

Joern Utzon, 38, of Hellebaek, Denmark, has won the £5,000 first prize in a world-wide contest for a design for a National Opera House to be built at Benelong Point.

His Opera House, estimated to cost £3,500,000, would have an unusual roof consisting of a series of shell vaults of cement covered on the outside with white tiles.

The judges, in their report issued yesterday, said: "Because of its very originality, it is clearly a controversial design. We are, however, absolutely convinced about its merits."

Controversy has already begun. One architect said last night that the winning design was "a piece of poetry . . . magnificent."

Another architect said the design looked like "an insect with a shell on its back which has crawled out from under a log."

"CHEAPEST TO BUILD"

Designed For Sandstone

Movable Walls Planned

How Long Did He Spend On The Design?

"One Of The Great Buildings Of World"

MR. J. UTZON

Other Stories On Design
● Conflicting Opinions—Page 3.
● Designers' Explanatory Notes—Page 3.

● Continued in page 3

PHONE TALK TO WINNER

Mr. Joern Utzon, the Dane who won the Sydney Opera House competition, is overjoyed by his success.

● Second prize-winning entry by a group of U.S. architects.

● Third prize-winning entry by a firm of English architects.

LATE NEWS

New Liner On Proving Flight

DURBAN TEST

Fire, Flood Threats

Three States—N.S.W., Victoria, and South Australia—are threatened with bushfires, but northern Queensland is gripped by floods.

Boy Drowns After 25ft Fall In Pool

A 6-year-old boy was drowned when he fell 25 feet into a deep rock pool at Wahroonga yesterday afternoon.

Slid, Rolled Down Rocks

QLD. STUDY OF PETROL PRICE ORDERED

Rocket Range Talks Started

Woomera Longer Than U.S. Range

Six Players In Team For Tennis Tour

COLUMN 8

Granny

On Other Pages

New York gives cold shoulder to King Saud. (p. 3)

Backstage moves delay U.N. decision on Israel-Egypt. (p. 3)

Milkmen threaten stoppage over sick leave dispute. (p. 4)

Man returns to U.S. with Sydney children, goes into hiding. (p. 5)

City hairdressers and food sellers to be X-rayed. (p. 5)

Duntroon cadets who tried to save five from drowning awarded George Medal. (p. 6)

City Council moves for higher building limit. (p. 6)

Girl motorist charged with manslaughter. (p. 7)

ABOVE The front page of *The Sydney Morning Herald*, 30 January 1957.

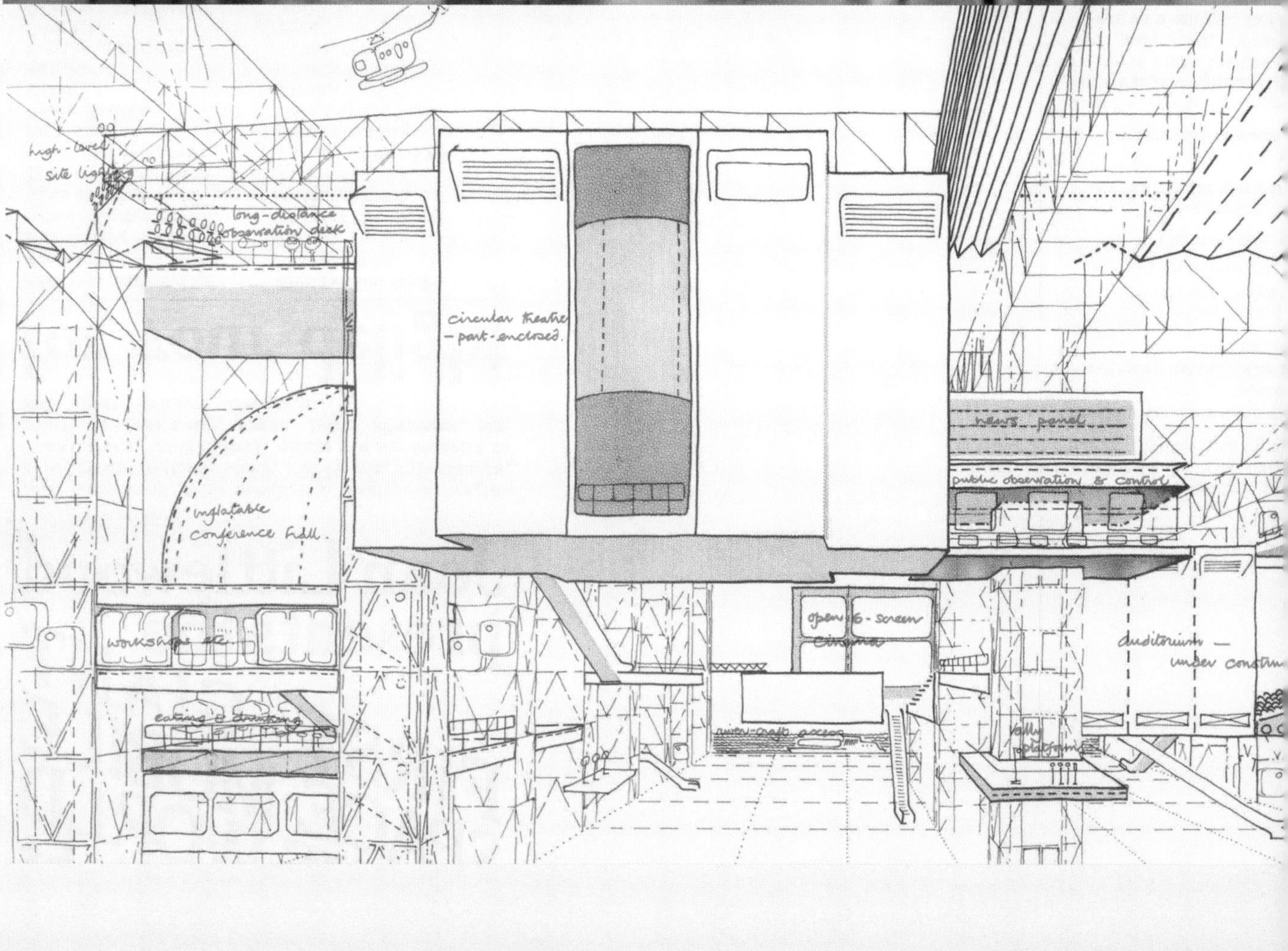
high-level
long-distance observation deck
circular theatre - part-enclosed.
news panel
public observation & control
inflatable conference hall.
open 6-screen cinemas
eating & drinking
river-craft access
valley platforms

FUN PALACE FOR JOAN LITTLEWOOD

LONDON, UK 1961

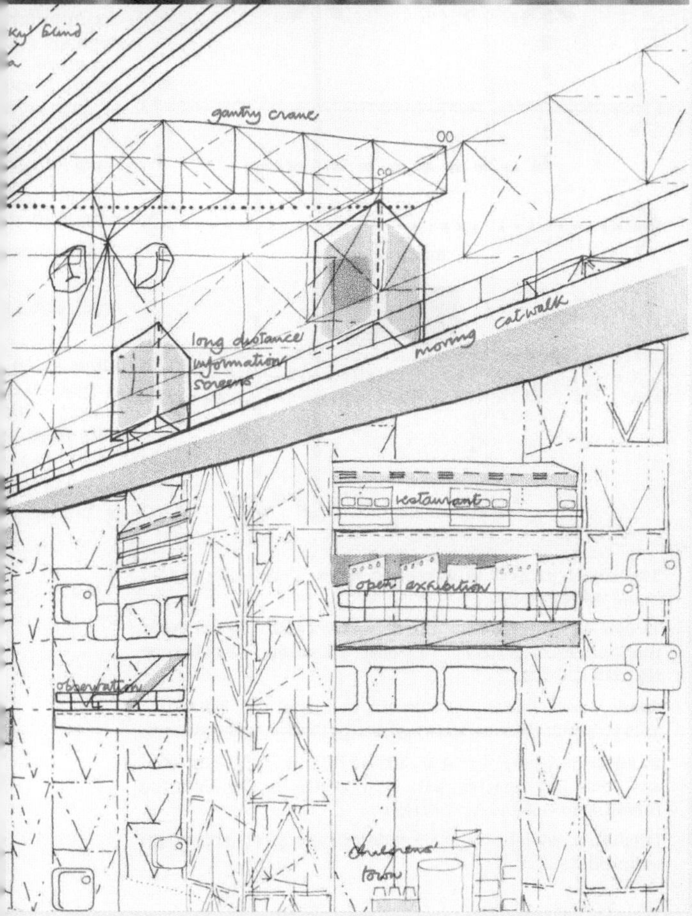

Joan Littlewood was a communist, prodigious actor and then director, who staged the first British production of Brecht's inspired and totally misunderstood anti-war polemic *Mother Courage and Her Children*, and set up shop at the Theatre Royal Stratford East in what is, despite having hosted the Olympics, still a resolutely working-class chunk of London that has resisted gentrification.

Cedric Price was an eccentric architect who'd worked under Lasdun and Goldfinger but pursued his own path – essentially one of flexibility and an aesthetic of, roughly, high tech. His Fun Palace for Joan would have taken the theatrics of Stratford one stage further by housing them in a giant structure which was to be endlessly adaptable and could host other events and arts organizations. He likened it to a kind of open-air shipyard of culture and pleasure.

A slimmed-down, working version of the idea called InterAction appeared at Talacre, next to the North London Line in Kentish Town, from the 1970s to the 1990s, but on a low budget. Hilariously, Price himself told English Heritage not to list it so it could be demolished – which it was. His ideas, we're told by numerous writers (and why should we argue with them), influenced Piano and Rogers's winning Pompidou Centre design and perhaps Will Alsop's ever so slightly car-crashy The Public in West Bromwich too?

A model (above) and drawing (left) of Cedric Price's Fun Palace for Joan Littlewood.

CONNECTIONS

‘LOMEX is …
automotive transit fetish
at its most decadent.’

UNKNOWN

MOTOPIA

STAINES, UK 1965

After the Second World War ended, Britain was in many ways a highly progressive country where nothing was deemed to be out of reach. From 1946, entire new towns were designated, and by 1959 many were well on the way to being completed – places like Stevenage, Harlow, Crawley, Peterlee, Basildon, Bracknell and Welwyn Garden City.

Geoffrey Jellicoe, architect and town planner, had masterplanned one of these new towns, Hemel Hempstead in Hertfordshire – though only portions of his plans there were eventually acted on. But as the 1960s were about to begin, Jellicoe had an even more ambitious scheme for a new town up his sleeve: Motopia.

This ruse had been funded by the Glass Age Development Committee, which claimed to be pushing for futuristic building techniques yet was funded by (wait for it) Pilkington Glass, and was essentially set up to try and flog as many panes of the transparent stuff as they possibly could by getting architects to draw up plans which required glass. Lots of it.

Jellicoe, a mild-mannered sort, had come up with a city made out of one giant 10-storey-high superblock running in up-and-down rows like a noughts and crosses grid. The walls would (naturally) be clad in glass. But the real shocker here was putting the roads on the roof. Ramps at the ends of the blocks would raise traffic from ground level, then it would circulate around Motopia on motorways in the sky. Heaven help you if your bedroom was a few feet beneath the carriageway.

But we're splitting hairs. In the 60s anything would be possible! As a Pathé news report confidently stated, 'The ceilings of homes below would be insulated against traffic noises.' Well, that's that then, nothing to worry about. Further plans show cars descending spiral ramps at the roundabouts where the axes meet and parking at car parks within the structure of the building.

Considering the huge amount of pollution all these clapped-out Morris Oxfords and Ford Anglias would have churned into the air (remember, this is the era before emissions standards), it's perhaps surprising to note that Jellicoe was more known for his bucolic garden designs than his town planning *per se* – indeed, the imaginary landscaping of Motopia looks lush and verdant.

Jellicoe was adamant that the whole idea was about giving people the freedom to enjoy nature

PREVIOUS PAGE Model of Paul Rudolph's LOMEX plan for New York.

LEFT Motopia, showing rooftop roads.

and banishing cars away from the ground. Although it sounds like a bizarre idea, land near Staines in Middlesex, south-west of London, was identified and there appears to have been some will to build Motopia at what was an adventurous time for town planning. However, it's apt that Motopia would have been within spitting distance of the great modernist laureate J.G. Ballard's house at Shepperton. You can imagine Ballard thrilling at Motopia, if it had ever been built – before immediately devising some kind of catastrophic situation for a future novel involving cars crashing off roofs and inhabitants driven crackers by the noise of a motorway just above their heads.

Plan Obus showing
connectivity in Algiers.

PLAN OBUS

ALGIERS, ALGERIA 1930-42

What was going on in Le Corbusier's head when he dreamt up the notion of rebuilding Algiers with, as its centrepiece, a giant 30-metre-tall superblock stretching the littoral length of the Algerian capital and topped with a poisoned crown – an expressway? In addition, of course, to a rebuilt business district with Plan Voisin-style skyscrapers linked by a high bridge over the Casbah, and a residential zone in the hills of something like a prototype of Niemeyer's curvaceous and overscaled Edificio Copan. In *Bidoun* magazine, Brian Ackley wonders whether Le Corbusier had spent too much time ogling the local ladies and had suddenly become enamoured of the curve? Like Picasso, he was taken with 'native' art and its exoticism. That's a by-product of colonialism, and so is trying to redevelop a city you never even owned in the first place – the Pieds-Noirs like Albert Camus, and the sadistic military 'protectors' who were depicted in the movie *The Battle of Algiers*, were kicked out of Algeria in 1962 at the successful conclusion of the independence revolution. Niemeyer, by the way, ended up there six years later, feted as a communist of course, building educational and civic structures.

Le Corbusier's plan was grandiose (*obus* meaning 'shell/shrapnel') and a probable inspiration for Jellicoe and others: the enormous bus stations in Beirut and Tel Aviv with huge interiors and serpentine rooftop access roads seem redolent of all this too, but they don't stick residential buildings under the elevated roads. Those resi units look a lot like the maisonettes that appeared, somewhat set back as if plugged in, in the Unité d'Habitation in Algiers' twin town of sorts – Marseille, the link between France and Africa. Except the roof there is crowned by a running track and pool – quiet, calm and cool. Le Corbusier was desperate to get Obus pushed through, even banging the drum for it to Marshal Pétain's anti-Semitic and vicious Vichy puppet regime (but then that's architects – they never look at the signature on the cheque, just check there is one) right into 1942 when war raged and no one in Algiers cared.

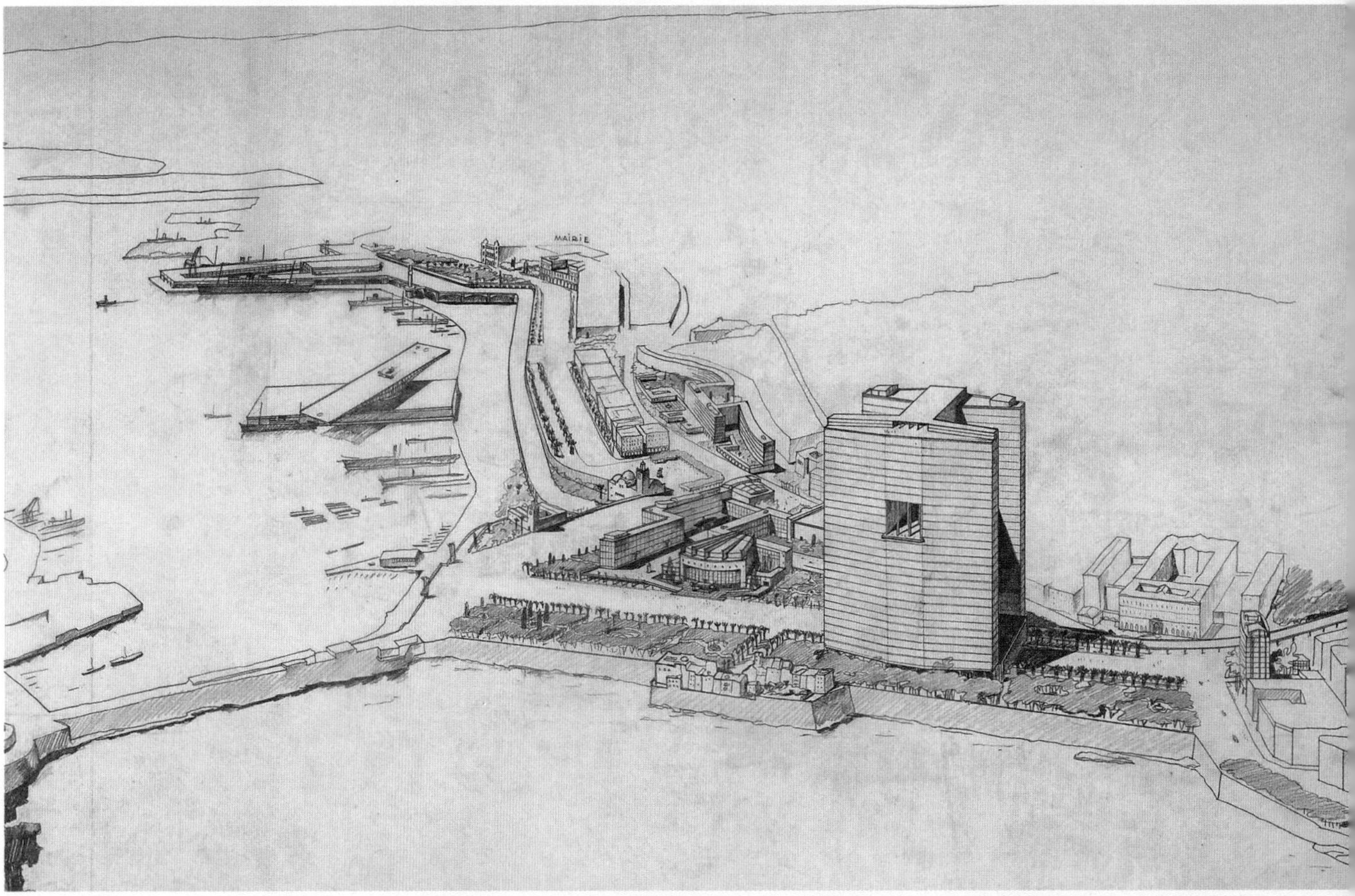

The Plan Obus for Algiers.

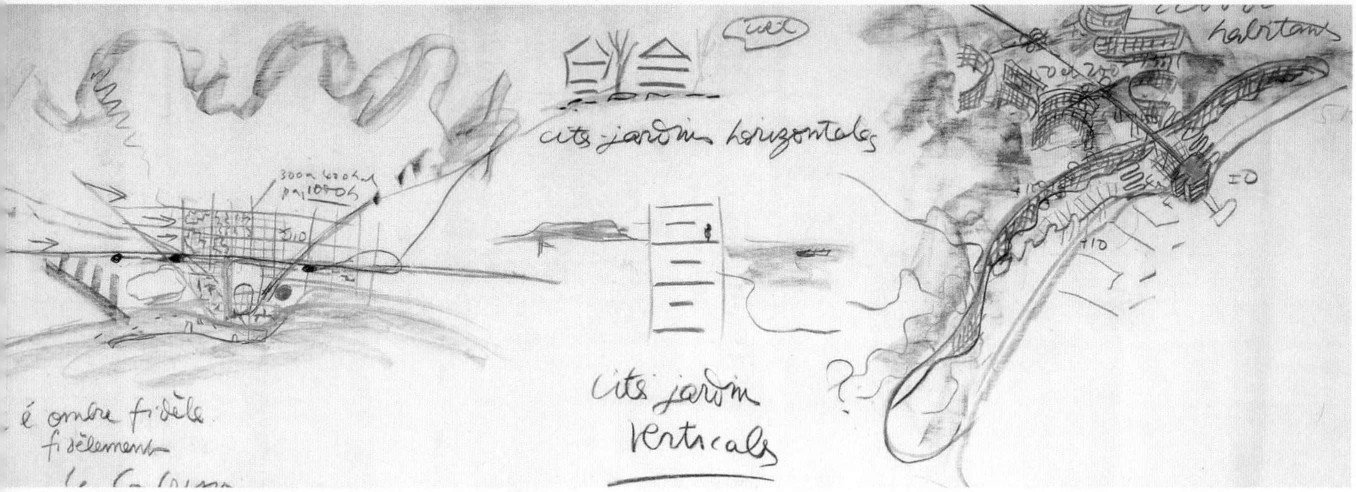

TOP Plans for Algiers, along with plans for a project in Barcelona, shown during a lecture Le Corbusier gave in Chicago in 1935.

ABOVE Le Corbusier's vision for the future of Algiers.

LEEDS LEVELS

LEEDS, UK 1960s

Leeds had previous when it came to envisaging something spectacular – and then not acting on it. In the 1930s the City Engineers Department dreamt up the idea of a pre-metro tram, essentially sinking tram lines under the streets, with a connection node for all the lines beneath City Square. City Square would later become the heart of a semi-realized council dream – this time for pedestrian transport. The city's skywalk was partially built from the Boar Lane shopping centre, across Park Row, skirting Infirmary Street, Russell Street and Greek Street. There were several entrances to the skywalk: ramps, stairs and – my personal favourite because I remember travelling on it as a child with my grandma in the early 1980s – an al fresco elevator up from Boar Lane to the shopping levels.

Other British cities adopted this approach and there are few reminders of it left: in Liverpool, Bristol and Newcastle the overhead walkways have mostly been erased. But this skywalk in Leeds was intended to be even longer – all new buildings had to have an upper-level entrance to connect to the skywalk and the Bank of England building still has these unused upper entrances.

But it got crazier still, because the Leeds planners wanted to connect all parts of the city centre, keeping the pedestrian level the same. So as the ground rose to the north the skywalk would become a subway system. When I went to university in Leeds the subways around the Merrion Centre began to be closed off – you could still peer down into them and spy the adverts for breakfast cereal or cars from years ago. But the fun didn't end there, because Leeds wanted to renumber every level of the city – from 0 at City Square to 18 at the top of the hill on which the university stood. Floors at the university hold to this rule and freshers today are still baffled about how level 7 or 9 can be the exit to ground level from different campus buildings on the steep

The Leeds skywalk is visible here along the front of the Bank of England building.

slope. The sloping site of the university was taken into account when Chamberlin, Powell and Bon masterplanned its 1960s expansion. CPB worked closely with the council on instigating this numeric levelling as well as getting a bridge built over the A58M/A64M inner ring road – Britain's first urban motorway – which sliced between the university and the city. Leeds at the time proudly called itself the 'Motorway City of the Seventies' – how times change. CPB also colour-coded each level after mapping the contours of the university site – so the infamous Red Route skywalk corridor, one of the UK's longest – corresponds to the point where the red contour hits the ground, before carrying on off into space, as the slope descends, ending up high above the ground.

In the end the city's levels were never renumbered *en masse* and much of the skywalk around City Square has disappeared – but look up on Infirmary Street and you can still see rogue doors and pointless terraces associated with its short life from the 1970s to the early 1990s.

LEFT The skywalk visible along the front of the Bank of England building.

OPPOSITE The skywalk running through City Square.

The skywalk crossing Park Row between the NatWest and Norwich Union buildings.

Cottingley
6304

MONDAY–FRIDAY
FROM 7AM–3PM
BREAKFAST & LUNCH

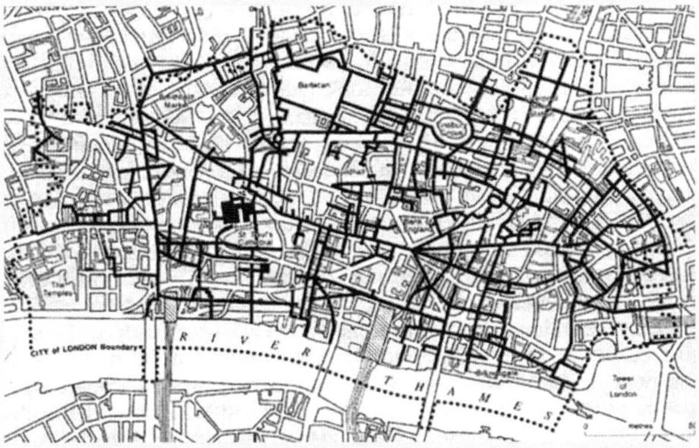

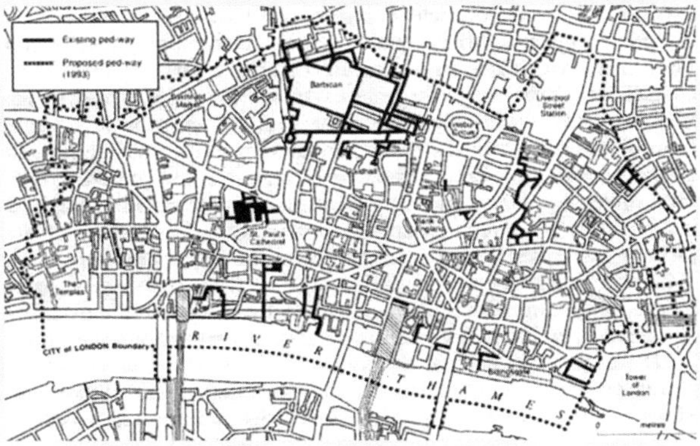

PEDWAYS

LONDON, UK 1950s-60s

The City of London's Pedway Scheme was proposed in plans by Charles Holden and William Holford, and would have criss-crossed the Square Mile. Very little of it was built; even less of it survives. But some of it does. As a trainee psychogeographer, aged about 13, I remember a school trip to the Museum of London and being blown away by the elaborate walkways and sunken gardens incorporated into Powell and Moya's 1976 museum and plaza. From a point on the pedway up here you can look down at no fewer than four levels, including the Ironmongers' Hall, peeking into view. The museum came at the end of the London Wall building boom which began in the 1950s and which saw the most of the pedway action, with a famous pub – the Plough – being one of the few landmarks people could find.

Yet there was no overarching plan – each developer was responsible for different sections. This is the heart of capitalist London, after all – the Square Mile has its own City of London council and police force. The Barbican (whose own deck is a relative oasis of calmness, paved in brick and only partially dislocating) did come to pass as a Gesamtkunstwerk, but from Christopher Wren onwards, full city planning in the City of London never really worked as a totality. So huge parts of the pedway were never built, while many office blocks were built with the stubs and connections for future paths that never arrived.

The unexpected postscript to the story comes on a sunny day during the Covid-19 crisis, when I found myself once more exploring the pedway and came across a fresh section that went up when Make Architects built a new office block next to the Salters' Hall in 2018 and installed a gleaming, serpentine new section of St Alphage Highwalk, which snakes around and under the new block, providing a Barbican connection and on which sit handsome benches. The magic never died.

TOP The original plan to have pedways criss-crossing the streets of London.

ABOVE The built pedway network as it existed in 1992.

OPPOSITE A new section of pedway in London, part of the London Wall Place redevelopment by Make Architects.

RINGWAYS

LONDON, UK 1960s-1973

Imagine walking through London's Camden Town. But instead of eccentric markets and giggling tourists, there's an eight-lane motorway soaring on concrete pylons above a windswept wasteland. Or Dalston: no hip bars and warehouse conversions, just a gigantic spider's web road junction which has obliterated everything. Or Highbury: no delis or pubs – a great slab of grey trunk road instead.

In the late 1960s, London was within a whisker of getting these motorways, and more. If the planners had had their way, they would have wrought more destruction than the Luftwaffe could manage during the Second World War. The London Ringways project would have been the largest single construction project in British history.

The problem: the post-war authorities feared that car ownership was getting out of control, and that the streets would soon be gridlocked. The plan: to ensnare the capital with circular motorways like a beast that needed taming – and then build more, penetrating from every point of Britain right into the centre of the city.

I became intrigued while living in Shepherd's Bush. I wondered why there was a section of motorway 1 mile long that didn't go anywhere. This road was known as the West Cross Route. At either end, Holland Park and White City roundabouts have slip roads, suggesting the motorway would have ploughed on north and south through dense housing. It turns out this was the plan; a small part of a monumental undertaking, described by Ringways expert Chris Marshall as 'probably ... the single biggest item of public expenditure ever proposed'.

There had been ambitious plans to give London a new road network earlier in the century. Engineer Charles Bressey and architect Sir Edwin Lutyens knocked heads together in the 1930s, but the Second World War got in the way of their plans. After the war, Britain's most famous town planner, Patrick

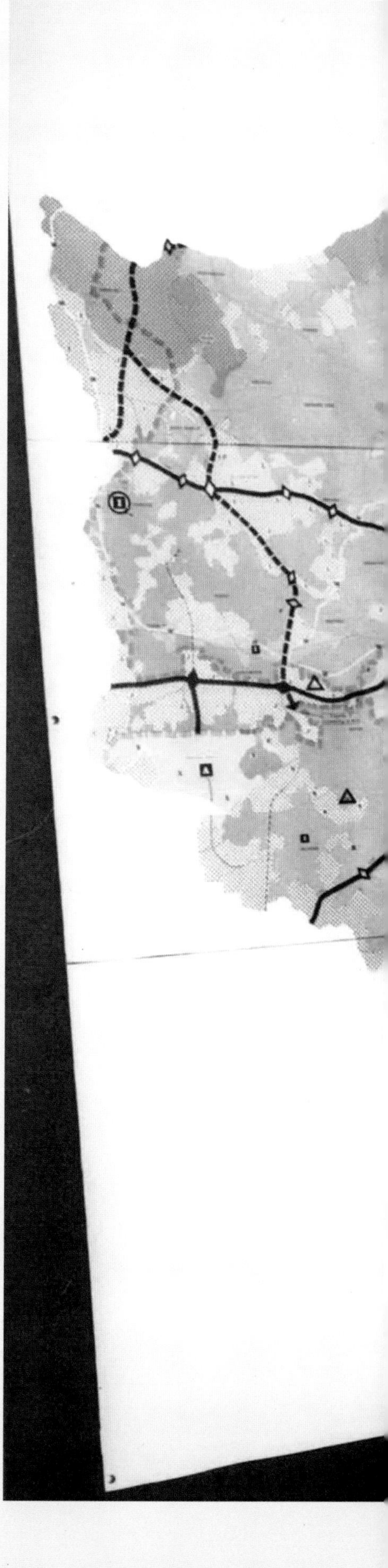

In 1969 RIBA produced a report, discussed at this press conference, arguing with the GLC's Ringways scheme, which would have involved mass demolitions.

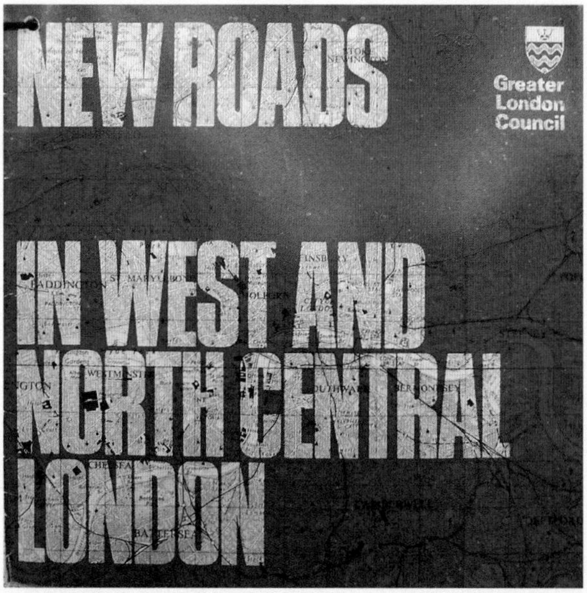

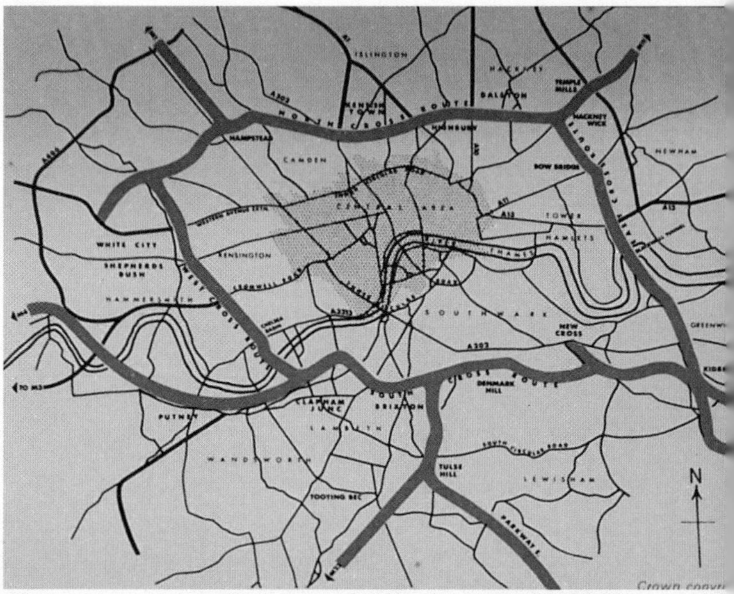

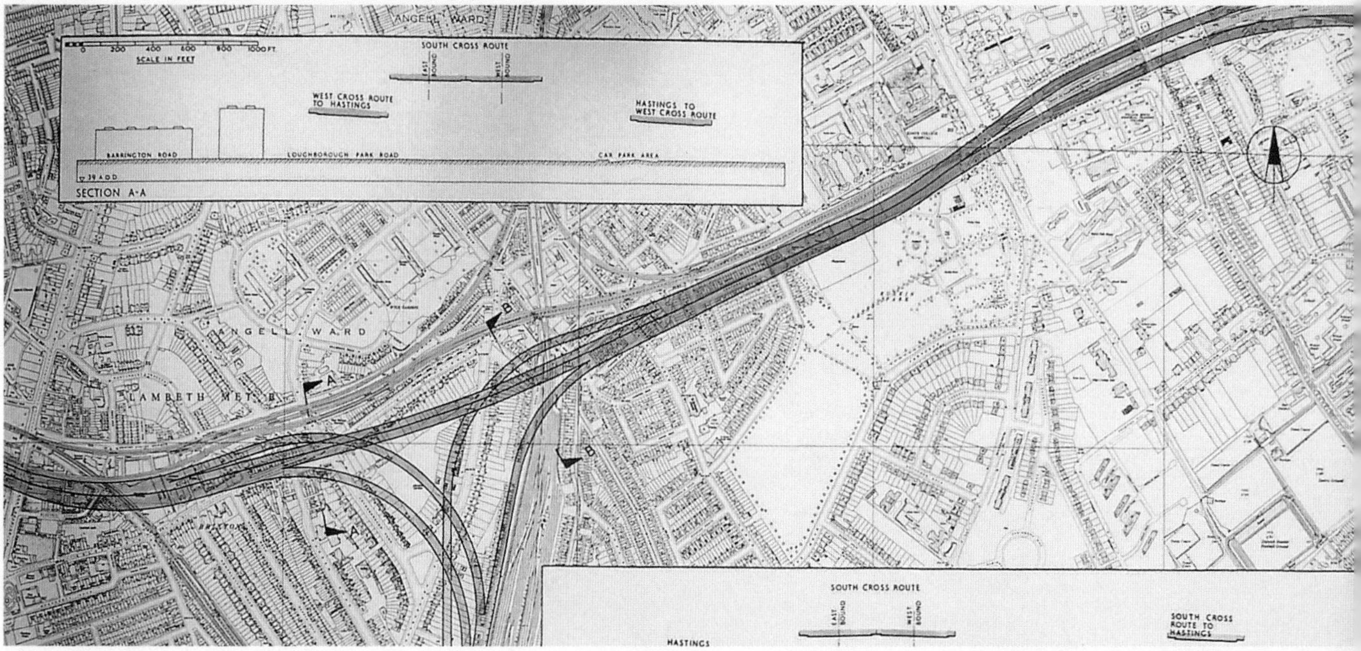

TOP LEFT Cover of the Greater London Council proposal, 1960s.

TOP RIGHT The proposed 'Motorway Box' (Ringway 1).

ABOVE The proposed South Cross Route slicing through Brixton.

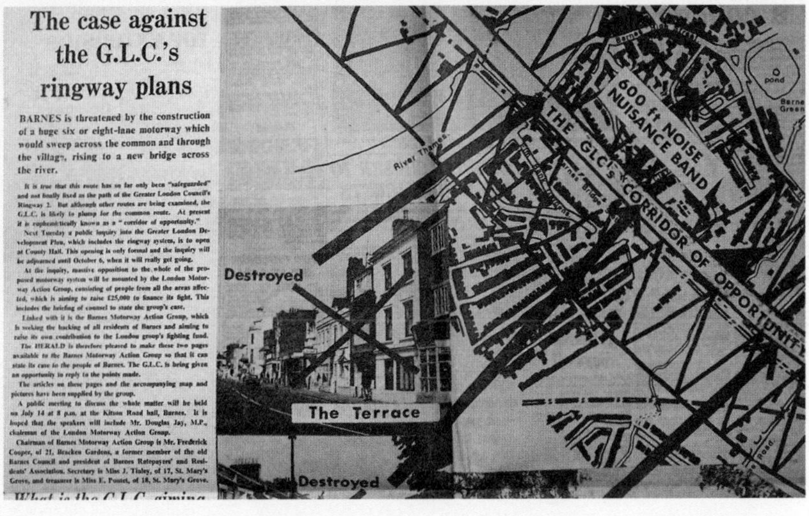

The case against the G.L.C.'s ringway plans

BARNES is threatened by the construction of a huge six or eight-lane motorway which would sweep across the common and through the village, rising to a new bridge across the river.

It is true that this route has so far only been "safeguarded" and not finally fixed as the path of the Greater London Council's Ringway 2. But although other routes are being examined, the G.L.C. is likely to plump for the common route. At present it is euphemistically known as a "corridor of opportunity."

Next Tuesday a public inquiry into the Greater London Development Plan, which includes the ringway system, is to open at County Hall. This opening is only formal and the inquiry will be adjourned until October 6, when it will really get going.

At the inquiry, massive opposition to the whole of the proposed motorway system will be mounted by the London Motorway Action Group, consisting of people from all the areas affected, which is aiming to raise £25,000 to finance its fight. This includes the briefing of counsel to state the group's case.

Linked with it is the Barnes Motorway Action Group, which is seeking the backing of all residents of Barnes and aiming to raise its own contribution to the London group's fighting fund.

The HERALD is therefore pleased to make these two pages available to the Barnes Motorway Action Group so that it can state its case to the people of Barnes. The G.L.C. is being given an opportunity to reply to the points made.

The articles on these pages and the accompanying map and pictures have been supplied by the group.

A public meeting to discuss the whole matter will be held on July 14 at 8 p.m. at the Kitson Road hall, Barnes. It is hoped that the speakers will include Mr. Douglas Jay, M.P., chairman of the London Motorway Action Group.

Chairman of Barnes Motorway Action Group is Mr. Frederick Cooper, of 21, Bracken Gardens, a former member of the old Barnes Council and president of Barnes Ratepayers' and Residents' Association. Secretary is Miss J. [illegible], of 17, St. Mary's Grove, and treasurer is Miss E. [illegible], of 18, St. Mary's Grove.

ABOVE Protests against the Acklam Road section of the Western Avenue Extension (Westway), on opening day.

RIGHT An article about road protests from *The Putney and Roehampton Gazette*, 1970.

SOUTHWYCK HOUSE
Recycling
BJ57 DVC

Abercrombie, dreamt up another monumental vision involving wholescale redevelopment. Abercrombie was a man obsessed by the future, and no one was going to stand in the way of progress. His 1940s plans contained provisions for various motorways – including one zooming past Buckingham Palace.

When the Euston Arch was demolished for a new train station in 1961, it seemed that nothing was sacred any more. Other world cities got their motorways: Paris had its Périphérique, while Robert Moses was carving freeways through the Bronx at will. The Greater London Council's final assault on traffic jams was drawn up in secret and eventually published in 1966.

There were to be four concentric ring roads. The North Circular and the M25 were completed in the 1980s. But the innermost, Ringway 1 – dubbed the 'Motorway Box', even though it looked more like a parcel the postman had squashed to fit through a letter box – was the real Trojan horse: four interconnected motorways that would have caused 100,000 people to be evicted and changed the lives of millions of Londoners. The North Cross Route was to slice from Harlesden to Hackney, the South Cross Route from Clapham Junction to Kidbrooke, bashing its way through Brixton town centre, all of which was to be razed and replaced with 50 tower blocks. The two parallel roads would be joined up by the West and East Cross Routes to form one bulbous, eight-lane ring road.

The Westway – London's most famous urban motorway – was also part of the plans. When it was being pushed through North Kensington from 1964 to 1970, grass-roots protest movements emerged and politicians got cold feet about building copycat motorways. In 1971, opposition movements coalesced into the London Motorway Action Group. It was the very start of the road protest movement.

In 1973, due to a combination of bad publicity, public disapproval and rising costs, the Ringways project was finally put to the sword. But traces remain. Keen urban archaeologists need only venture to Hackney Wick to see the Ballardian concrete island of trees between the carriageways of the A12 at Mabley Green, which would have been slip roads in a huge free-flow junction. At Brixton the 'Barrier Block', AKA Southwyck House, stands as a sturdy reminder of the Ringway – it was built specifically to face and face off against the new motorway, protecting the flats behind it.

Southwyck House, Brixton, still standing today and known as the 'Barrier Block', was to have faced the Ringway and acted as a noise baffle to protect local residents.

CA 973-035
NJ 14012

CAPE TOWN FORESHORE FREEWAY

CAPE TOWN, SOUTH AFRICA 1977

Cape Town accidentally left itself with an icon when it failed to complete its Foreshore Freeway in 1977, leaving two stubs that have featured in numerous films and TV shows, and the photographs of thousands of visitors. The money ran out after South Africa's 1960s boom (predicated on racism and the toil of millions of low-paid black workers) petered out and the freeway along the waterside was simply not finished.

In a postscript to the story, yet another plan was concocted around 2018 for the freeway to be completed and intense high-rise residential development to slotted in around it, but this too failed due to economic uncertainty. So the now-renamed roads of the two great anti-apartheid heroes – Helen Suzman Boulevard and Nelson Mandela Boulevard – still remain unconnected. Other cities also had these incomplete 'ski jump' ramps, coming off their own incomplete urban motorways too: like Seattle, Portland, Glasgow and Manchester.

The section of unfinished freeway, Cape Town.

BERING STRAIT CROSSING

SIBERIA, RUSSIA TO ALASKA, USA 1890s-PRESENT

From 1890 until today a crossing of the Bering Strait has been dreamed of, mapped out, planned out, mulled, debated at length. Why? There's nothing on either side of the Strait – for hundreds of miles. This is not a no-brainer link between Malmö and Copenhagen or under the English Channel. Zoom out, though, and you'll see the significance of linking together essentially all the world's land masses. You could drive from the southern tip of Chile, or anywhere in the Americas connected by road, to any point in Asia, Europe or Africa. Put a railway in and you have the possibility too for moving massive amounts of cargo – including fossil fuels mined in the Arctic. It's a delicious prospect, though of course one that horrifies environmentalists.

Various proposals to build bridges or tunnels over, through and under the Diomede Islands have been floated throughout the twentieth century and more recently too. Political stumbling blocks – this would cross the border between the USA and Russia – and more prosaic ones too, like having to build hundreds of miles of road and rail through the harshest and coldest conditions on Earth just to link up to each end of the crossing, have dogged progress.

Other stalled fixed-link crossing proposals include Germany to Denmark over the Fehmarn Belt, Morocco to Spain, and Sicily to the Italian mainland. But don't rule out any of these civil engineering super-projects – they could come back to life. The first of these, Germany to Denmark over the Fehmarn Belt, for so long an unbuilt project, finally seems to be happening. Even Northern Ireland to the UK may be on the cards in the bizarre post-Brexit world.

Map showing the Bering Strait between Russia and Alaska.

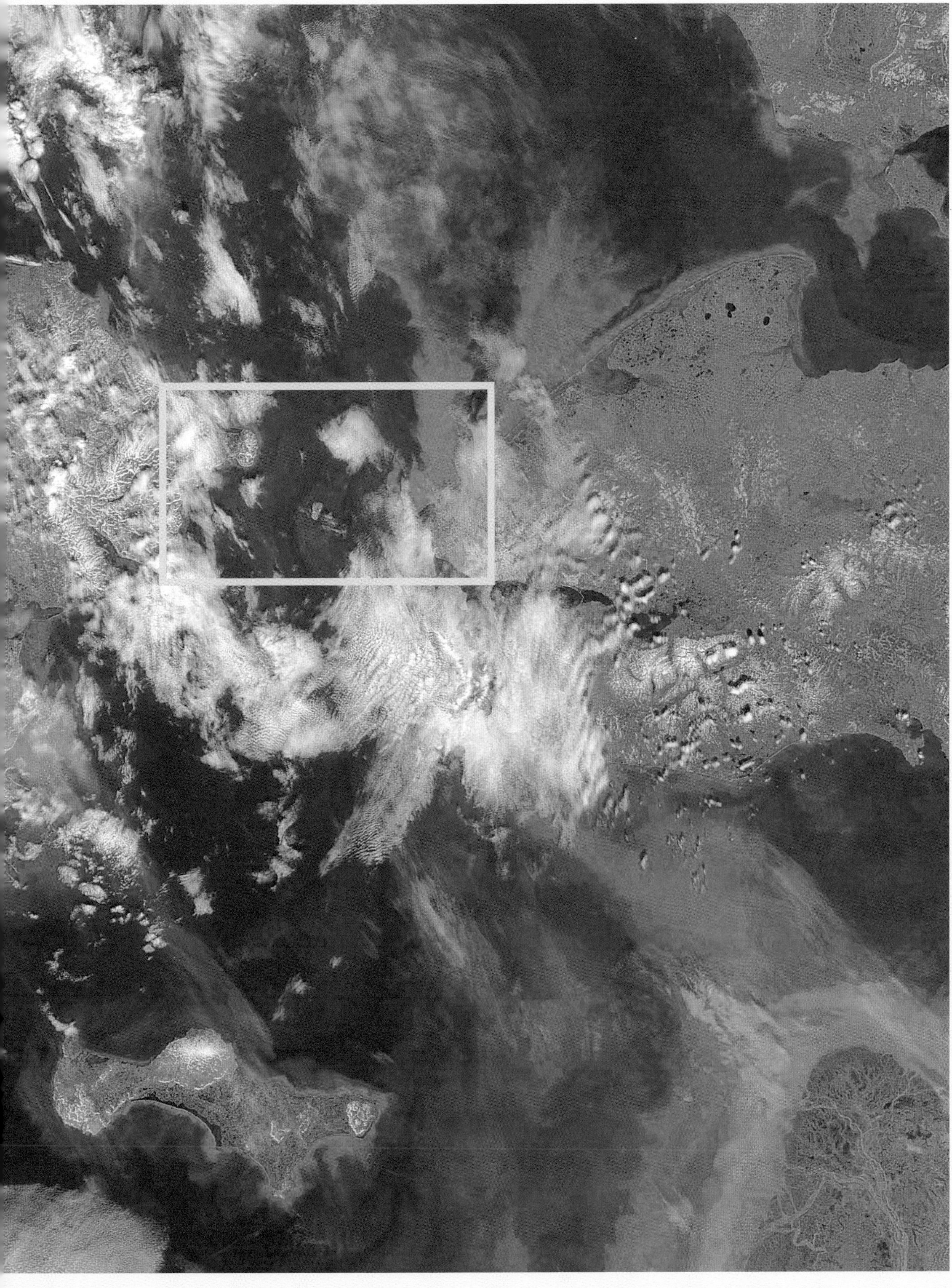

LOMEX

NEW YORK, USA 1967-71

The plan that – perhaps – sunk modernism once and for all, the Lower Manhattan Expressway (LOMEX) was cancelled in 1971, the year before the Pruitt-Igoe towers began to come down in St Louis, and so that was that for an era. Hands rubbed together, right? But LOMEX is really a tale of two plans.

The bad cop is Robert Moses – the slash and burn megalomaniac (and, many would argue, racist) who wanted to redraw New York in his image, succeeding to some extent. Yes, he updated the city's creaking infrastructure – but at what cost? The devastation wreaked by the Cross Bronx Expressway – on, let us not forget, Hispanic and black neighbourhoods, was a taste of the firestorm a freeway across Lower Manhattan could have brought. It's no wonder the journalist and activist Jane Jacobs objected. Her primal scream against *grands projets* struck a chord with many who were

RIGHT Model of Paul Rudolph's LOMEX, wide view with transit hub.

BELOW Robert Moses with a model of LOMEX.

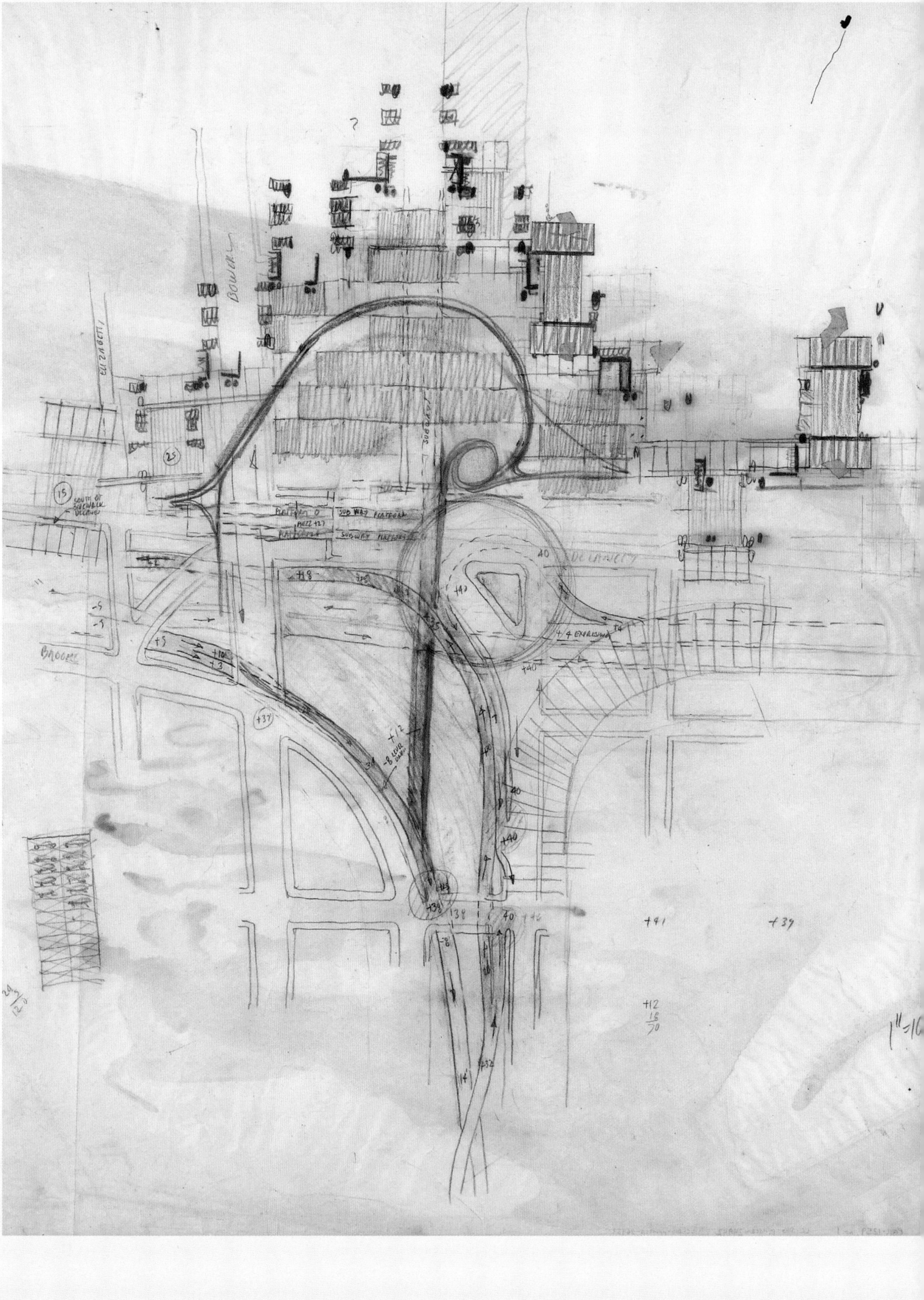

sick of the redevelopment, who wanted to go back in time rather than forwards somehow. Jacobs became an icon for a growing movement of anti-modernists who held sway – especially through the 1980s and 90s when the crosshairs suddenly became fixed on any brutalist building in particular: anything with a deck, anything with levels, anything made of concrete.

The good cop (notionally) was Paul Rudolph, thoughtful architect of such modern treasures as Boston's Government Service Center (itself intriguingly incomplete and devoid of a planned tower and, as of 2021, threatened with demolition) and the Yale Architecture Department in New Haven. His LOMEX scheme came late to the party in 1967, attempted to ameliorate the worst excesses of the freeway, and put on top of it a superblock so distinctive that it was used as the cover image for Reyner Banham's 1976 book *Megastructure*. Rudolph's way with a pen and pencil brings the ideas to life: the A-frame above the sunken roads, the ascending flight of towers, the stepped balconies, the monorails under the roof of the Hub dome. Here, the grandiose comes with an implicit elegance; concrete comes with poise, a vision with some style. If only we could have somehow had Rudolph's wild theatrics, but without sacrificing Soho and the Lower East Side. Maybe the plans as a product in and of themselves are what's really of note here?

OPPOSITE Sketch plan of the LOMEX transit hub.

BELOW Bird's eye perspective drawing of LOMEX.

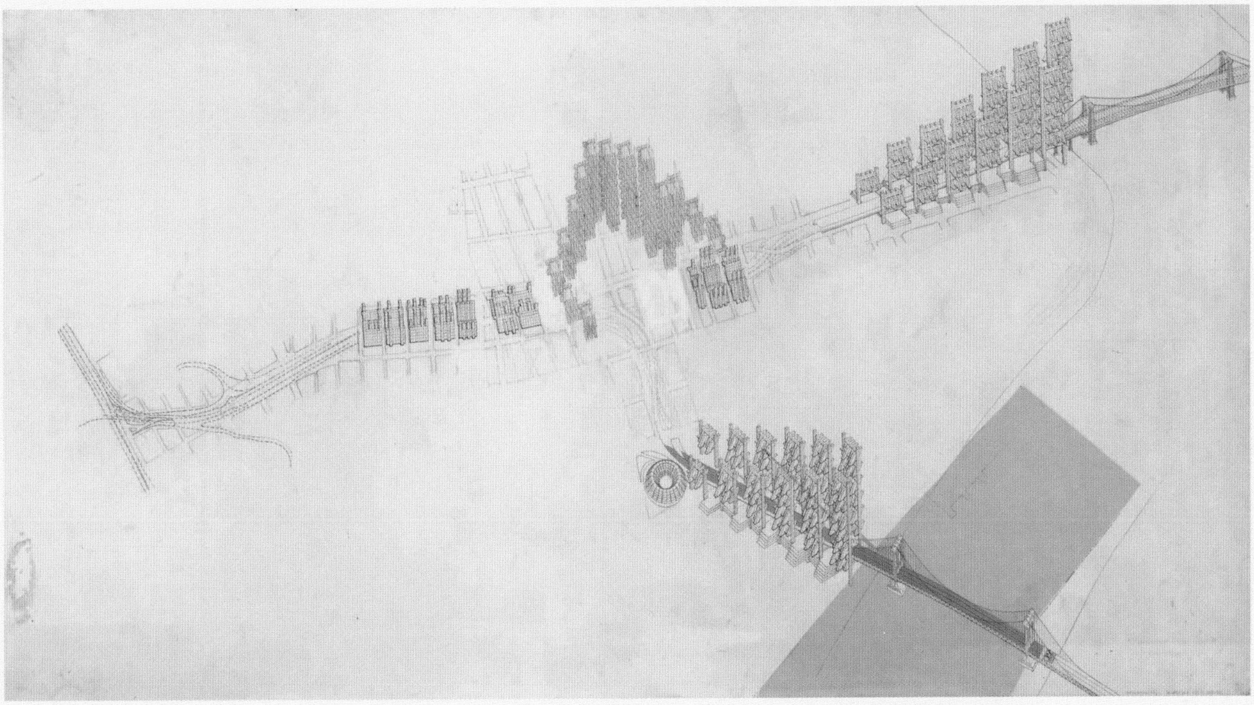

ABOVE AND OPPOSITE Inside the superstructure that Paul Rudolph envisaged.

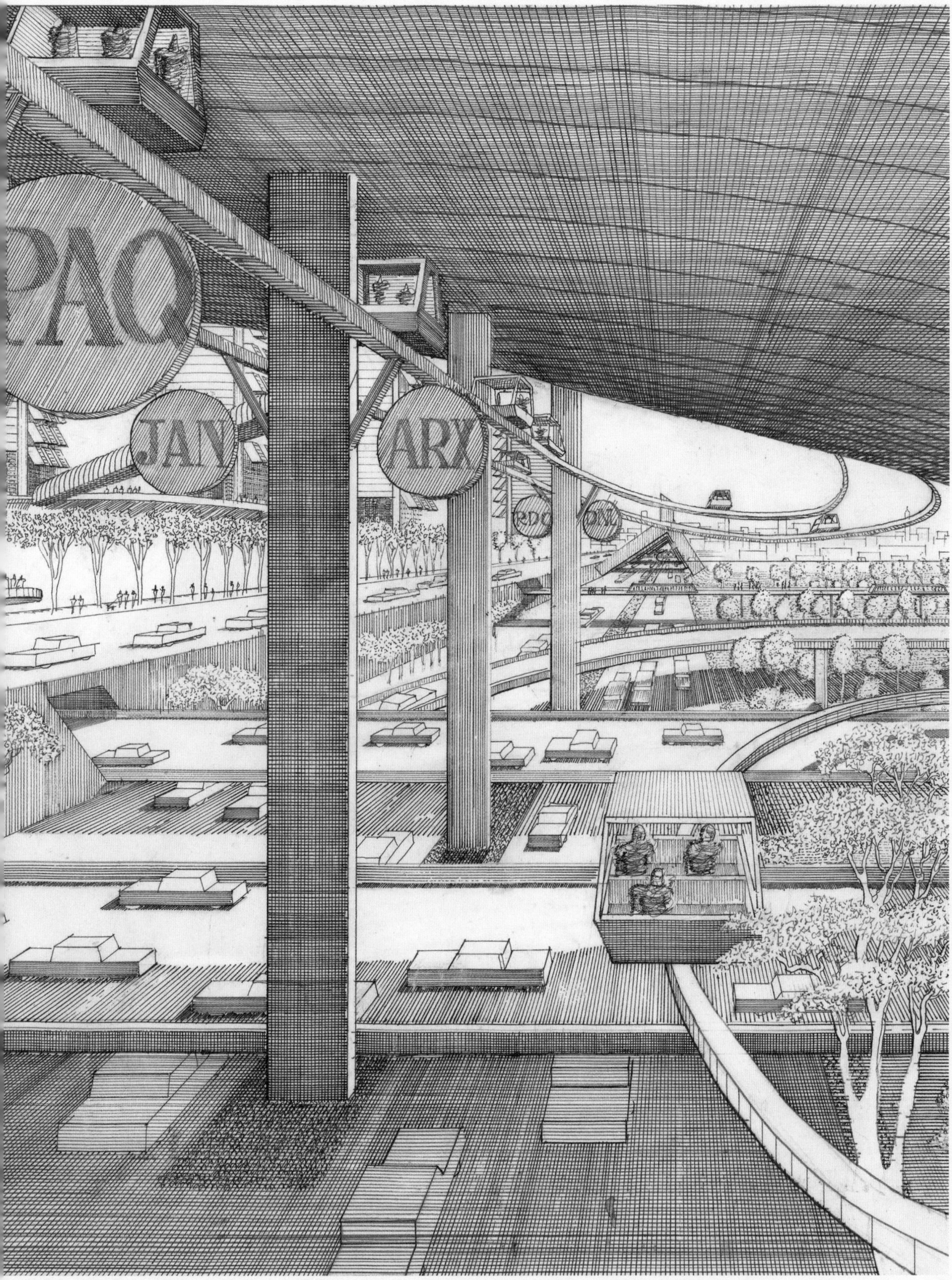
PAQ
JAN
ARX

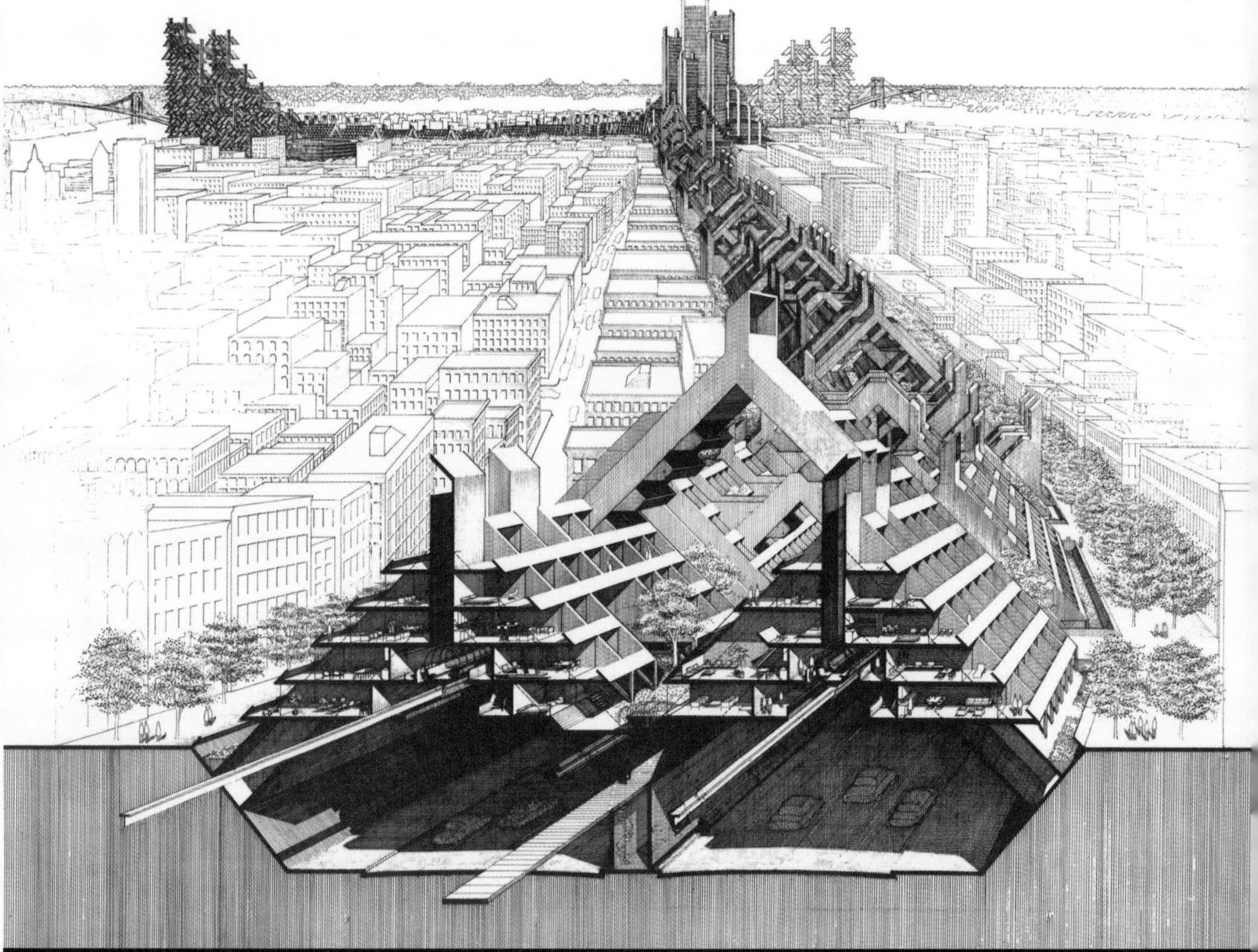

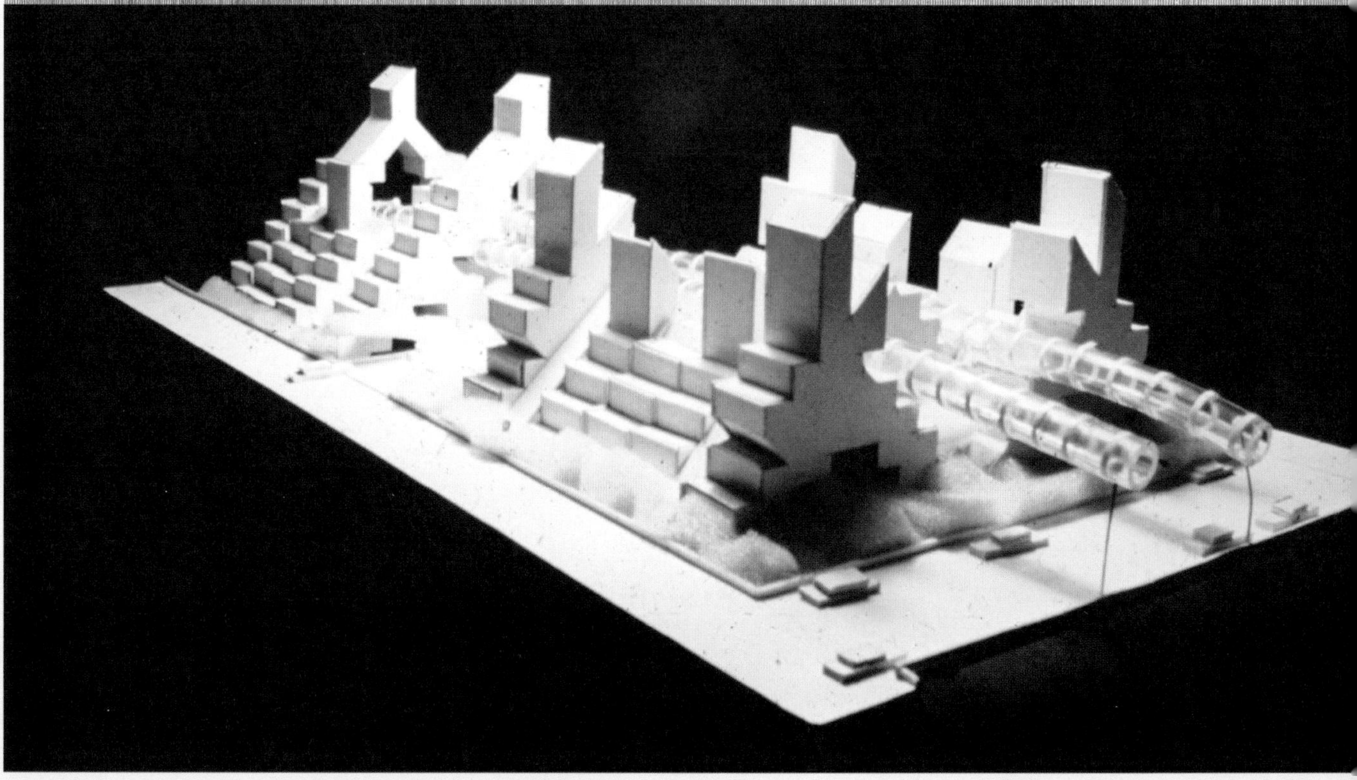

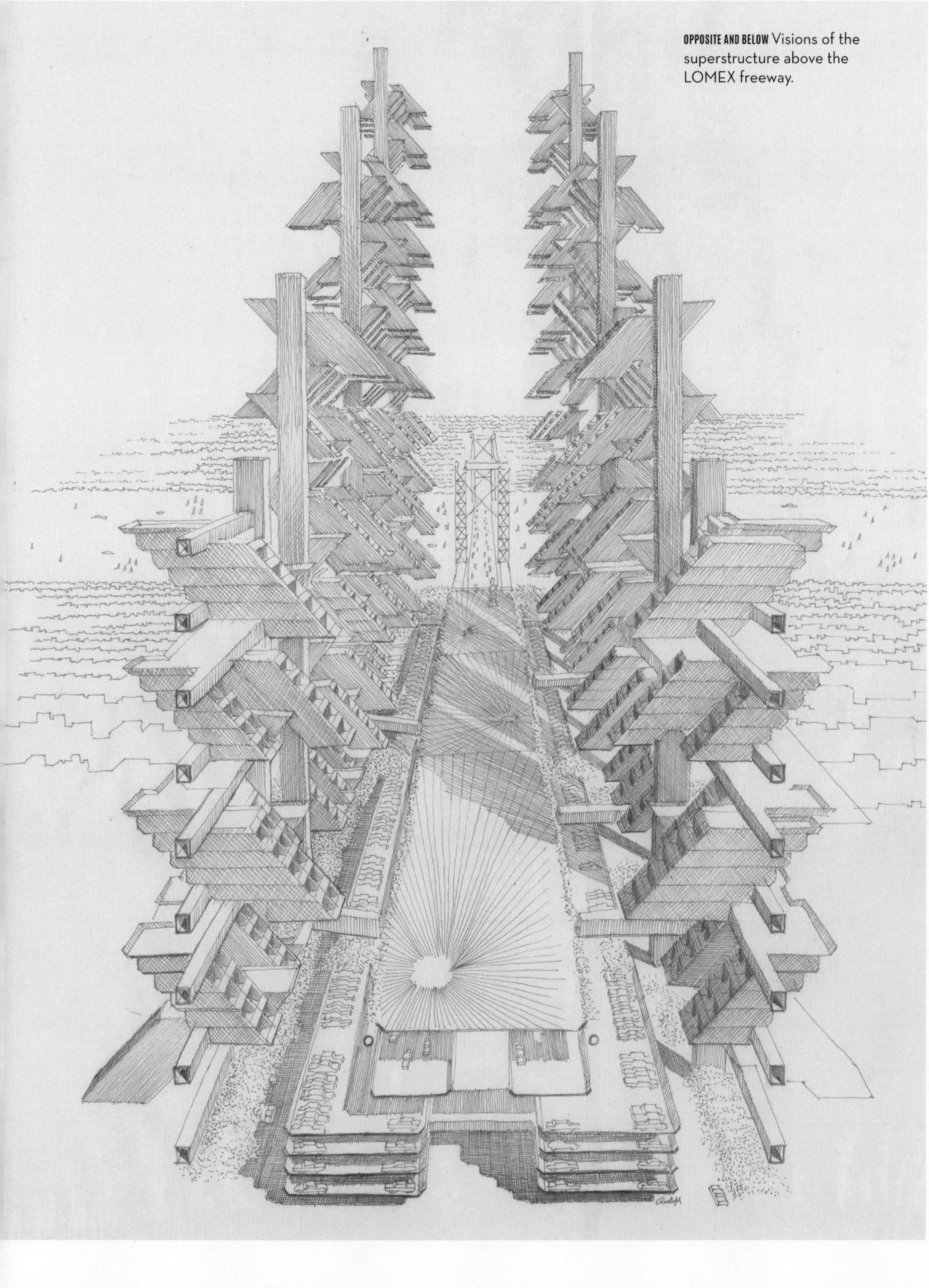

OPPOSITE AND BELOW Visions of the superstructure above the LOMEX freeway.

REPRESENTING UNREALITY: COLLAGES, DRAWINGS, VISIONS

The question of how to depict what is yet to be there has weighed on the minds of architects since their profession began.

Drawings were the way architects worked before computer-aided design became as ubiquitous as fake tan adverts on Instagram, and in the hands of the skilled the pencil could bring a world to life, like Paul Rudolph's gripping visions of the LOMEX superblocks looking very Kubrickian indeed.

Montage gave that Fritz Lang flourish: Mies van der Rohe's Friedrichstrasse Skyscraper in Berlin (1921) comes alive when compared to the earlier charcoal rendering, likewise El Lissitzky's Cloud Irons (1925) placed on to the Moscow cityscape to look as dramatic as a Chekhov play.

Illustrations brought colour and life to visions, saying quickly what might not have been so readily understood in the text of seminal books like *Traffic in Towns* (1963), which were pushing at the limits – and whose vision of a multi-layered Fitzrovia with escalators and decks had to be seen to be believed. Colour made the concrete seem less austere and the radicalism less threatening; it's a truism – points out Jonathan Glancey – that blue and yellow umbrellas appear as a constant trope, recurring over and over again in these multitudinous illustrations, with 1960s hepcats sipping martinis under them, waiting for a Bond baddie to arrive. The same could be said of the woman pushing a pram through a park – a figure that is almost unavoidable in architects' depictions of social housing to come, for example. The imagery and ideas behind this symbolic new life are clear enough. David Gosling's illustrations of an imagined future for the new town of Irvine in Scotland have a delicious Ballardian quality to them, with DeLorean-esque cars racing underneath brutalist hotels. His bold use of blue as the sole colour, added to iconographic simple signage, simmers up a soup of strange singularity, as if we're heading for a future colony on a moon of Saturn.

Collage is perhaps the most interesting of these tools. For Golden Lane (1950s), those wacky Smithsons put Gerard Philipe outside in the garden and Joe DiMaggio and Marilyn Monroe inexplicably up on the deck about to go into their flat ... for a cuppa? With Civilia (1971), Hubert de Cronin Hastings placed recognizable existing brutalist buildings like Habitat 67 and London's Queen Elizabeth Hall over a natural landscape of an Albion populated with slightly baffled-looking punters coming from a Nuneaton Town football game. There were also boats everywhere: sailing, boats and water – another one of those tropes one sees as often as a politician lying. The water was so ubiquitous in the firmament that Anthony Burgess wrote the 'flatblock marina' into his 1962 novel A *Clockwork Orange*, which probably encouraged Stanley Kubrick to shoot that famous droog fisticuff scene on the banks of Southmere Lake at Thamesmead, a rare vision of a fantastic future that came true – and has since been totally taken apart and replaced with 'ironic' CO decorations like retro lettering and orange fences (LOL) around the Southmere Marina Boathouse.

Dieter Urbach's 1960s collages are some of the most mesmerizing. Is that a blue and yellow Regenshirm? Of course it is, with hot girls lounging outside a huge residential megastructure by a Spreewald lake – it's like a modernist drinking game. The women seem snipped from a state-sanctioned fashion mag. There's a jollity to this image, which was used as a main poster for the Berlinische Galerie's exceptional exhibition 'Radikal Modern'. Museum staff tracked down the recluse Urbach, who had neither a phone nor email, and got hold of his originals – other works show DDR *grands projets* like Alexanderplatz looking rather more bleak in black and white but with these intriguing cut-out people scattered throughout.

Archigram went wild with collage, even producing their own magazines full of pop images which fizzed and banged, always including bright colours, models, bold lettering and *homo ludens* getting pissed or playing sport – these images brought to life the Instant City idea and the plan for the Monte Carlo Palm (a summer casino, 1969) especially well.

Latterly computer-generated images have inevitably shown projected buildings in an intensely eerie kind of dusky sunlight, like something from a video game – always with an excess of plants to display their tiresome 'green' credentials. Meanwhile, a recent wave of realistic 'what if' computer montages have illuminated the likes of the runners-up in the Sydney Opera House competition, showing what could have been.

FORM BAR
AURANT

HYPERMODERN MOVEMENT

'The future became easy to recognize because it had monorails in it.'

REYNER BANHAM

KING'S CROSS AIRPORT

LONDON, UK 1931

It's taken a very long time for King's Cross to be seen as a solution rather than a problem. Today, London's dynamic post-industrial district brims with cranes. The postcode N1C was created in 2010, and now the area is home to new flats, restaurants, Central St Martins college, one of Britain's most respected media companies, *The Guardian*; and will soon host Google's UK headquarters in their futuristic 'landscraper'.

For hundreds of years King's Cross was synonymous with sleaze, as one of London's most notorious red-light districts, and urban deprivation (see the streets coloured black on Charles Booth's poverty maps). The creepiness of the place persists today in some of its back streets and yards. A young Thomas Hardy had a job supervising the movement of graves at St Pancras Old Church when the railways ploughed through the whole area in the 1860s. Bodies were snatched for medical experiments too.

That same spirit of slash and burn practised by the railway engineers is evident in the 1931 King's Cross Airport plan by architect Charles Glover, who put forward the idea of installing eight runways over the district's skyline, an urban airport in the shape of a cartwheel accessed by lifts. He wouldn't have dreamt of suggesting such a thing over the buildings of Mayfair – but King's Cross was a place where it seemed just fine. It was certainly visionary. In the 1960s, Glover had another crack with a plan for a new Covent Garden vegetable market at King's Cross, topped with what every 1960s building really needed – a heliport.

Few cities in the world have been as airport/heliport mad as London. In the 1930s London considered an airport on top of skyscrapers in Liverpool Street, on the Thames itself, and even on the South Bank between London Bridge and Tower Bridge. The Southbank Centre was also suggested as a venue for a heliport in the late 1960s, and this is one reason why the Hayward Gallery and Queen Elizabeth Hall have such unyielding, tough and windowless exteriors – the architects thought they'd have to fight against aviation noise.

PREVIOUS PAGE Foster + Partners' SkyCycle proposal.

OPPOSITE Charles Glover with his model for the King's Cross Airport.

Despite Heathrow Airport being built in the far outskirts of west London, the city has struggled with air capacity in the twentieth and twenty-first centuries, and in the 1970s plans were made to build a new airport at either Maplin Sands off the Essex Coast, or at Cublington near modern-day Milton Keynes. Neither materialized.

In the end, an airport at King's Cross, so near to central London and so whimsically fashioned, was too much to swallow. But the idea of an airport in the Thames Estuary persisted. In the 2000s, airports that could replace Heathrow were proposed at Cliffe, or off the Isle of Grain (the latter was a Norman Foster plan). And then of course there's the infamous 'Boris Island', a plan for an airport at Shivering Sands named in dubious honour of former London mayor and UK Prime Minister Boris Johnson, who pushed for it.

The closest relative of the King's Cross Airport plan (that actually got built) is London City Airport in Docklands, which opened in 1987 on a spur of land between two docks in the city's east. It's extremely popular with business travellers today because of its proximity to Canary Wharf and the City. However, it has a whiff of thoughtlessness in the way locals are treated (and would have been treated with the King's Cross Airport) because this is not a deserted area – there are streets and estates housing thousands right up against the airport's southern boundary in Silvertown, and for them it's a noisy co-existence.

Only a few short years after Glover's King's Cross proposals, Berlin got a new terminal at the airport bang in its centre, though – the legendary and legendarily large Zentralflughafen at Tempelhof, now decommissioned and an interesting relic and park. The motif of helicopters and planes landing on top of buildings would recur in piles of 'futuristic' architectural proposals for half a decade to come.

Drawing of the airport above King's Cross Station.

MPRESSIONISTIC SKETCH OF —
AILWAY - ROAD GOODS TERMINUS
DISTANCE COACH & CITY OMNIBUS STN.
& AIR PORT.
T KING'S CROSS - LONDON.
ULTING ENGINEERS & ARCHITECTS. J. STANLEY WRIGHT. ASSOCIATED ARCHITECT.
PATENT APPLICATION

SHEFFIELD MINITRAM

SHEFFIELD, UK 1975

Sheffield could have had a Minitram in 1975 but instead, 20 years later, it got a Supertram (one spelling mistake there and the council could have accidentally paid £240 million for a 70s prog-rock band). The Minitram project was masterplanned by RMJM, and showed citizens exactly what they'd be getting via a series of doctored photos that depicted the small 15-person cars trundling over such local sights as the infamous 'Hole in the Road' roundabout on an elevated guideway. The system looked extremely similar to the type you see operating between terminals at airports like Orlando, Zurich, Gatwick and Stansted, with each vehicle being very small and probably using wheels on tracks, though perhaps with more traditional rails.

The eventual Supertram (just a conventional modern tramway) took a very similar route but mostly at ground level, rather than on a high viaduct, while a similar low-usage personal rapid transit (PRT) system was installed at the University of West Virginia in Morgantown. London also mulled a Minitram scheme from Croydon to New Addington, but this too later reappeared as a conventional tram. The Docklands Light Railway (opened 1987), meanwhile, bore certain resemblances to the Minitram project with its elevated tracks and automated vehicles, though they were much larger.

LEFT Booklet explaining the ambitious Sheffield Minitram project.

OPPOSITE The Sheffield Minitram passing over the notorious Hole in the Road roundabout.

Bovis
YORKSHIRE BANK
M&M
COMMERCIAL SPARES
SHEFFIELD

AEROPORT MIRABEL

MONTREAL, CANADA 1970s

Today Aeroport Mirabel is a ghost town, its flying facilities ostensibly reserved for cargo planes and for the Bombardier aircraft manufacturers based nearby. For 30 years from 1975 there was an airport here – but it was just a tiny taste of the planners' real intentions. By surface area, at the time Mirabel was the world's largest airport. In an effort to prepare Montreal for both the 1976 Olympics and a glittering future to come after (oops), enormous swathes of rural Quebec were expropiated. The aim was to build a mega-airport like Dallas/Fort Worth with an incredible six terminals and six runways, way more capacity than would be needed for decades. One terminal was built in smoked glass by Papineau Gérin-Lajoie Le Blanc and flights were accessed by the Plane Mate mobile-lounge concept, jacked-up buses that trundled around like something from *The Jetsons* and only ever made it here, Washington Dulles and a few other airports (these could themselves form a part of our discussion about broken dreams, for they were meant to usher in a different future). Rail and road infrastructure was never properly completed for Mirabel and the distance from the city caused huge headaches.

Montreal's existing airport at Dorval is now its premier gateway once more. The terminal at Mirabel has been bulldozed but the culty, brutalist Chateau de l'Aeroport Hotel opposite stands forlorn for the time being, a memory of a vision that, like the '76 Olympics, didn't quite work out as well as Montreal's rather more architecturally successful Expo '67, with its lasting works by Buckminster Fuller (The Biosphere) and Moshe Safdie (Habitat 67).

Aeroport Mirabel's sprawling site, showing how far the airport was meant to spread.

ABOVE Inside the terminal at Mirabel that was built.

OPPOSITE, ABOVE The exterior of the terminal.

OPPOSITE, BELOW The terminal being demolished.

MAGLEV

GERMANY, JAPAN, CHINA, SOUTH KOREA, UK, FRANCE 1960s-PRESENT

Birmingham's airport isn't like other airports. Right at the north-western end of the runway there's a country park and a row of benches. You'll see families picnicking here, enjoying the subsonic spectacle of planes from Brussels, Bucharest and Barcelona roaring just overhead on their final approach. Birmingham isn't like other British cities, either – it fetishizes the technical and promotes the new. It is unstinting in its thrall to evolution and unsentimental about erasing past versions of the future in its rush to create new ones; the comprehensive 1960s vision of the city which itself swept away a century of Victoriana is currently being meticulously taken apart, concrete slab by concrete slab.

When you get to a certain age you realize how much more visions of the future say about the present they're concocted in than the actual future they purport to show us hurtling towards. A track in the air, sitting on top of concrete legs that couldn't look any more like rational new humans striding into a technocratic promised land if they tried, will always evoke a kind of nostalgia for the twentieth century. You think of the SAFEGE monorail depicted in Truffaut's 1966 film adaptation of *Fahrenheit 451* and of regional news reporters with greasy barnets delivering excited pieces to camera about big plans.

Today, on the elevated track that gambols over windswept car parks and threads through cheap motels between Birmingham's airport terminal and the railway station, a simple, ski resort-style people-mover system ferries passengers from plane to train. Three decades ago it was so much more exciting: the world's first commercial maglev – magnetic levitation – system ran along here. Opened in 1984, the Birmingham Maglev came at the very tail end of a *trente glorieuses* for British transport technology and, more broadly, European

The M-Bahn, Berlin's short-lived maglev.

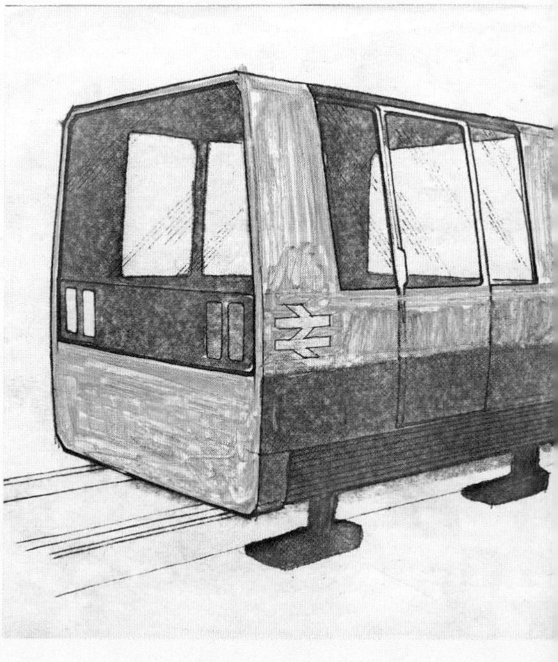

engineering; an era that promised so much yet eventually bequeathed so many relics and ruins.

The modernism of the twentieth century, expressed especially in architecture and engineering, seemed like nothing less than the founding of a new order. Progress was to be continual, unstoppable and good. Yet today the physical and philosophical advances are being gradually taken apart and retracted, as if we'd woken up sweating and feared we'd somehow overreached ourselves.

The maglev was a development that spun out of the British Rail Research Division, founded in 1964, and developed in a joint project with a private consortium that included the now-defunct General Electric Company. But the British maglev never really took off, lasting 11 years: maintenance costs for what was really a unique system were high.

You don't have to look far to find other relics of this white-hot time when post-war confidence begat all sorts of oddities. There's the test track for the French Aerotrain outside Orléans – a rocket-powered prototype that never made it to middle age. And in Emsland, the German conglomerate Transrapid built a 32km (20 mile) supersized test track for their maglev, which seemed to be on course for success. A variation of this train shuttles passengers from Shanghai and its airport, and the plan was to copy the same model in Munich, and even build an intercity line from Berlin to Hamburg.

Little remains of Germany's other maglev, the M-Bahn (or Magnetbahn), a short-lived shuttle service that ran in West Berlin from 1989 to 1991 connecting stations whose service had been previously severed by the Berlin Wall. With the Wall gone, the old U-Bahn service was reinstated and the M-Bahn, which had run along its tracks, disappeared from the capital of the new Germany.

In the Far East, attitudes to maglev are different. Japan began maglev testing at roughly the same time as Britain in 1962 and is today building the longest, fastest maglev in the world, scheduled to open in 2027. It will run mostly in tunnels, at 500km/h (300mph), taking a shocking 40 minutes to travel the 300km (200 miles) between Tokyo and Nagoya. It's been christened the Chūō Shinkansen: just another, faster type of bullet train for the central districts. Japan's system is different to the Birmingham and German systems, using superconducting coils in the train, which cause repulsion that moves the train forward. The Japanese also use wheels for the vehicle to 'land' on the track at low speeds.

The Chinese are building various intercity maglevs and proposing even more. South Korea likes them too. The deployment of maglev schemes in Asia is understandable, though, given the huge passenger numbers needed to justify the massive capital costs involved.

So there are still some people dreaming big. The latest iteration of this is Hyperloop, whose vacuum-tube technology harks back to another British engineering innovation: the atmospheric railway, which was developed by Henry Pinkus, the Samuda Brothers and eventually by Isambard Kingdom Brunel. This technology used varying air pressure to suck trains up a track in a partial vacuum. Lines popped up in London, Dublin and, most notably, Brunel's South Devon Railway, where the pipes were plagued by nibbling rats but the pumping stations survive as relics of Victorian visionaries.

If those systems looked like something from H.G. Wells, with men in top hats smoking cigars, then Hyperloop, with its internet-age funding from Tesla founder Elon Musk, could well end up appearing as a very 2010s caper when we look at back on it from the distance of decades. Or maybe Hyperloop will revolutionize travel like maglev was supposed to.

In the 2000s the UK Ultraspeed proposal was floated to link London, Birmingham, the North and Scotland by maglev. It never materialized. HS2 was the eventual successor to the Ultraspeed plan, though a less futuristic one.

How things move (sort of) full circle: intriguingly, part of the HS2 plan now calls for an elevated train to link the new Birmingham Interchange Station with the airport. Will it be a maglev? It should be – the Germans are once again mulling them; plans were floated in 2020 to link Berlin's new Brandenburg Airport to the city with one.

OPPOSITE, ABOVE The Aerotrain.

OPPOSITE, LEFT The Queen opens the Birmingham maglev, between the NEC and the airport, in 1984.

OPPOSITE, RIGHT British Rail's original design for a British maglev for Birmingham.

PLATFORM BAR
RESTAURANT

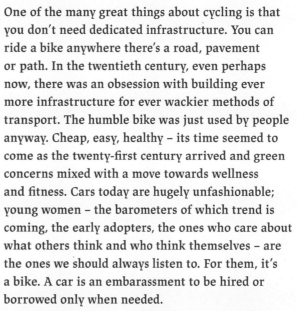

SKYCYCLE

LONDON, UK 2013

One of the many great things about cycling is that you don't need dedicated infrastructure. You can ride a bike anywhere there's a road, pavement or path. In the twentieth century, even perhaps now, there was an obsession with building ever more infrastructure for ever wackier methods of transport. The humble bike was just used by people anyway. Cheap, easy, healthy – its time seemed to come as the twenty-first century arrived and green concerns mixed with a move towards wellness and fitness. Cars today are hugely unfashionable; young women – the barometers of which trend is coming, the early adopters, the ones who care about what others think and who think themselves – are the ones we should always listen to. For them, it's a bike. A car is an embarassment to be hired or borrowed only when needed.

Cycling was always popular in flatter countries like the Netherlands and Belgium. Large intercity networks in Flanders and expansive cycle routes in Dutch cities made cycling a breeze. Some countries of late have wanted to catch up. London has experienced a cycling boom and a 2013 plan for the so called SkyCycle network would have slung wide cycle lanes above the main rail lines out of London.

The first proposed route would have run overhead from Liverpool Street through East London to Stratford, with ramps and even lifts from ground level up to the cycleway. The idea came from Foster + Partners, Exterior Architecture and Space Syntax, based on an idea by Oli Clark. Smaller elevated cycle routes do exist, like the Luchtsingel over the train tracks in Rotterdam and the Bicycle Snake above a Copenhagen waterway. And as Oliver Wainwright reminded us in *The Guardian*, there was once a plan for the California Cycleway – a route in the sky from Pasadena to Downtown LA. One section of it was in fact opened in 1900, but hasn't survived.

The SkyCycle project, running through East London.

ABOVE Elevated cycleway in Rotterdam.

RIGHT The California Cycleway, built in 1900.

OPPOSITE The Bicycle Snake bridge in Copenhagen offers a fun ride along the harbour.

NEW CITIES

'An engineer should not merely sit back and predict the inevitable end result of carrying on present practices. He should design the future.'

ATHELSTAN SPILHAUS

Bass
N BOTTLE
LIA

CIVILIA

WARWICKSHIRE, UK 1971

Britain's Brasilia? Nuneaton doesn't quite have the balmy climate of the Goiás plateau, but then both sites were widely regarded as unpromising – a slice of Brazilian cattle-grazing scrub and a few old quarries in the least pretty part of Warwickshire.

The idea present in a lot of planning and implicit in Civilia's wry nomenclature is that 'they' (the straight, white, middle-class and middle-aged male planners) could get 'them' (the working classes) to elevate themselves. Here was a kind of Thamesmeadean idea where, if you put enough marinas and fountains and lakeside promenades between the brutalist buildings, you could end up with – as Owen Hatherley has referred to Thamesmead – at least a 'working-class Barbican'.

Civilia: The End of Sub Urban Man is a call for urban Britain to be bold in a sense, not to succumb to the laziness of the semidetsian suburbs Ian Nairn mapped – but to build daring and high-density cities.

Architectural Review publisher Hubert de Cronin Hastings was being playful on some levels – choosing the *nom de plume* Ivor de Wolfe and using photomontage to elaborate, almost satirical effect, by glueing existing monuments of his era, like Habitat 67 in Montreal and the Queen Elizabeth Hall on London's South Bank, on to a landscape of bucolic British greenery, with the proletariat merrily strolling up staircases and peering over platforms at traffic below and monorails above. The presentation of the whole thing is its best quality perhaps – the fresh fonts and innovative visuals sort of satirical but with some of the same blithe spirit that accompanied much of these 1960s and 70s plans.

PREVIOUS PAGE AND LEFT Collages showing the vision for Civilia, mixing bucolic and brutalist.

PREVIOUS Hastings' vision of the university in Civilia.

ABOVE LEFT Vertical halls of residence for students.

ABOVE The 'university megastructure'.

'A perilous stair known as Jacob's Ladder' forms part of the Galleria area of Civilia.

DONGTAN

DONGTAN, CHINA 2005

An island at the very mouth of the mighty Yangtze was earmarked to become a new eco-city in 2005, and a huge one at that – housing, eventually, 500,000 citizens, but in some comfort and in a very different manner to some of China's megacities. Dongtan was supposed to be about greenery, technology, space, low-rise architecture and ecological solutions to modern urban problems. The development stalled despite the involvement of renowned engineering group Arup. It was supposed to be a showpiece 'living architecture' exhibition at the 2010 Shanghai Expo, where China wanted to show off its modern, global credentials. In the end all that exists is a bridge across the delta back to Shanghai, some roads ... and a bird reserve. Now the island will probably just be developed in a more traditional way without the green policies that it aimed for initially.

BROADACRE CITY

USA 1935

Broadacre City comprised elements of wacky futurism (helicopters-cum-flying saucers, somewhat incongruous super-tall skyscrapers and – as this was a suburban wheeze – highways) with pastoral, low-rise exurbs. In a sense, American cities cherry-picked certain elements of the design for the next half-century – despite Broadacre itself never being built.

Fly over any sunbelt suburbs and the shapes of the cul-de-sacs and the almost endless urban sprawl appears particularly piquant. The dream of 'an acre of land' is alive. Cars still dominate American travel, American dreams. Frank Lloyd Wright had higher aspirations than strip malls and fast-food joints, and sprinklers destroying the water supply. He was probably thinking about the English garden-city movement and about nature and humans finding an accommodation at a time when cities like New York – where the famous model of Broadacre City was displayed in the Rockefeller Center in 1935 – were much dirtier, less desirable places to dwell than they are today.

RIGHT Frank Lloyd Wright's vision of Broadacre City.

BELOW A colourful map of the proposed development.

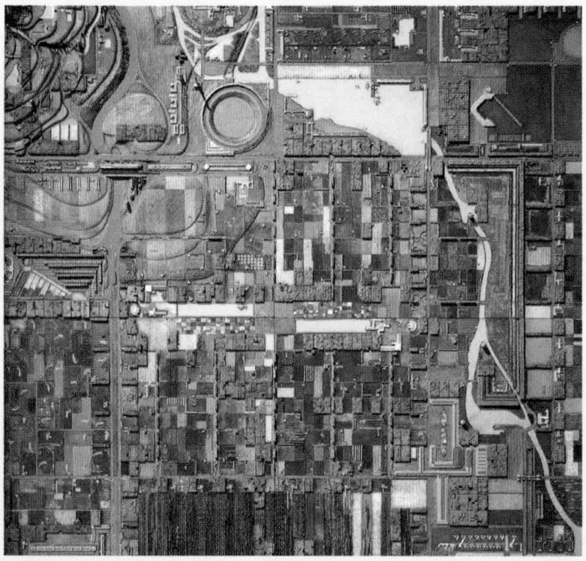

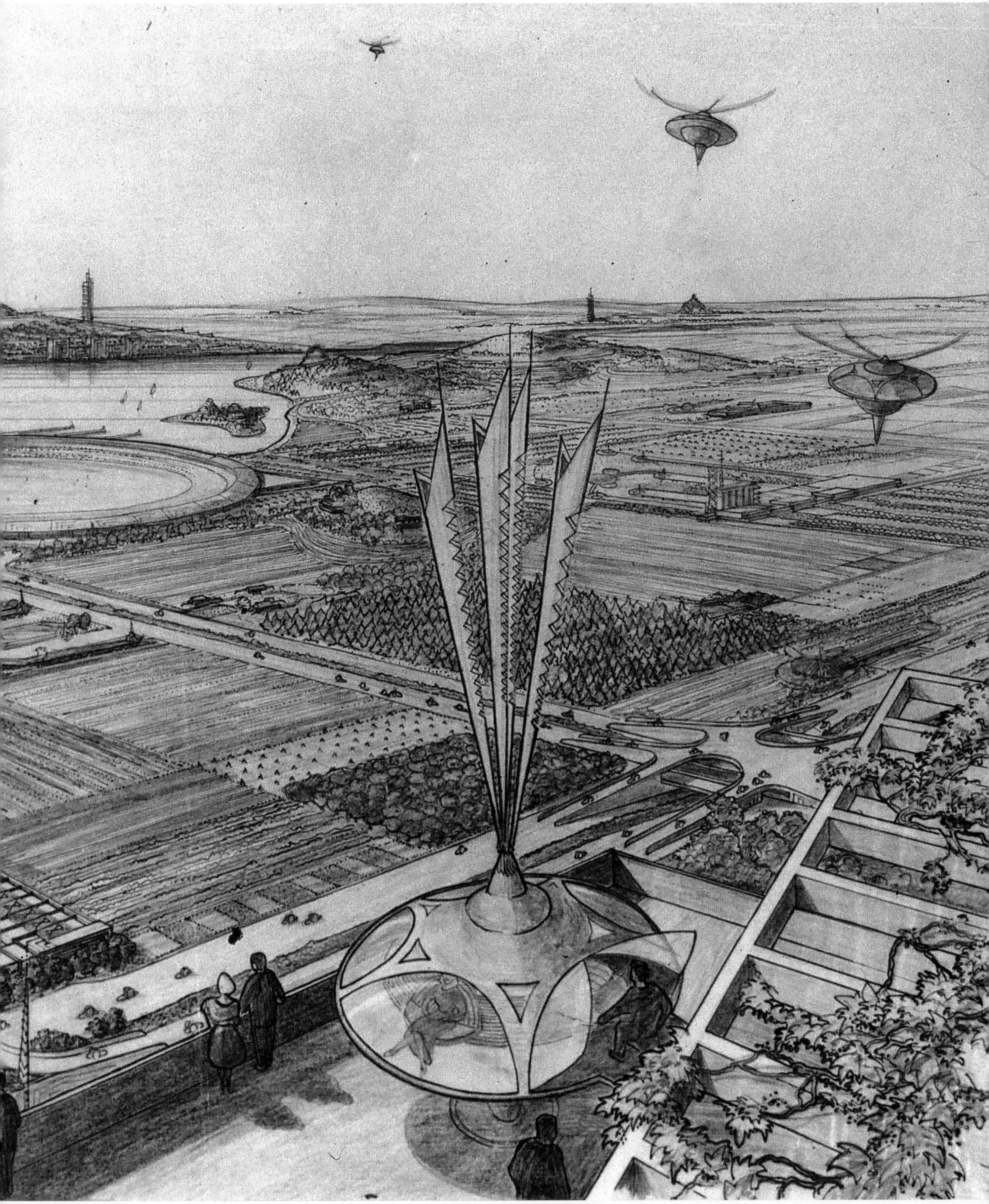

MINNESOTA EXPERIMENTAL CITY

MINNESOTA, USA 1966

The frankly bizarre story of the Minnesota Experimental City, with its *Blade Runner/Robocop*-esque corporate MXC logo, was told poetically in Chad Freidrichs's documentary *The Experimental City* (Freidrichs also made the excellent *The Pruitt-Igoe Myth*, which debunked much unfair criticism of the quality of those infamously deleted St Louis housing blocks). The story of MXC is a wild one – anchored by Athelstan Spilhaus, who surely must have been an influence in the mind of Conan O'Brien when he wrote the character of shyster monorail salesman Lyle Lanley in the classic *Simpsons* episode 'Marge vs the Monorail'. Spilhaus was heavily influenced by Buckminster Fuller and wanted to build a massive new city powered by a nuclear power station in the Swatara swamp in rural Minnesota, with a dome, nascent computer technology deployed widely, heavy private-sector buy-in, and tracks where your car would be controlled and you wouldn't have to drive. A revolt by locals managed to derail the ambitious plans.

OPPOSITE, ABOVE The charismatic dreamer Athelstan Spilhaus.

OPPOSITE Visions of how Minnesota Experimental City would come to life.

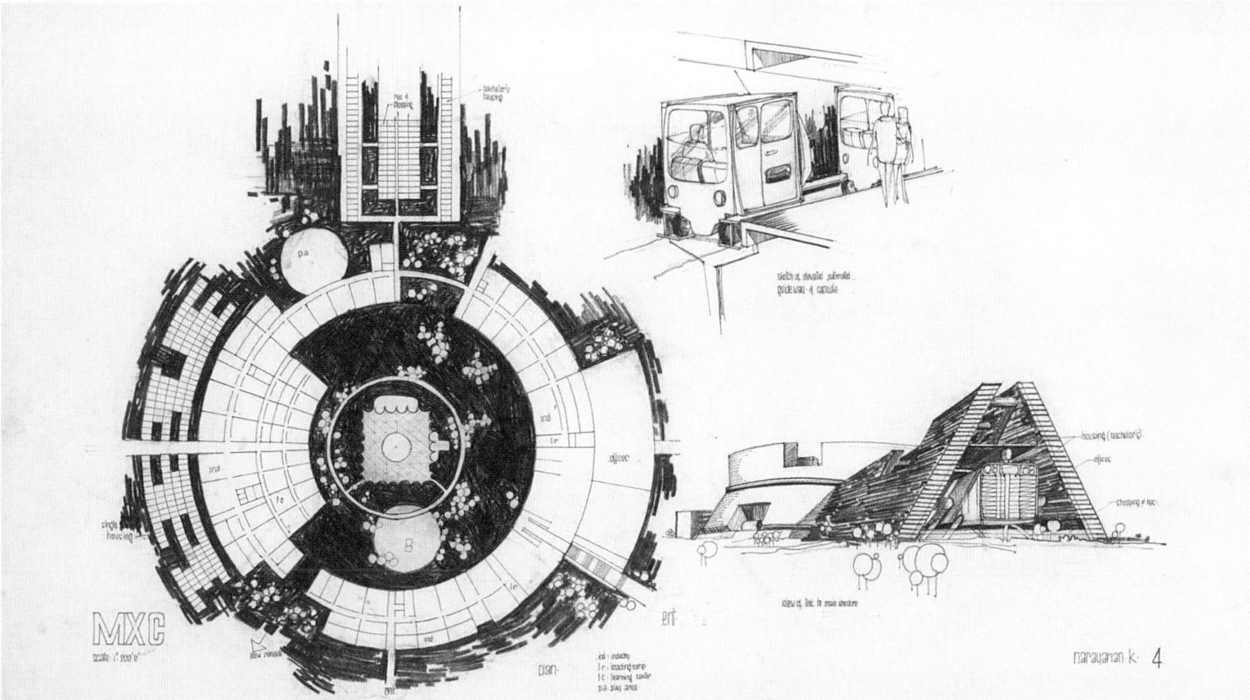
MXC
plan
single housing
office
narayanan k. 4

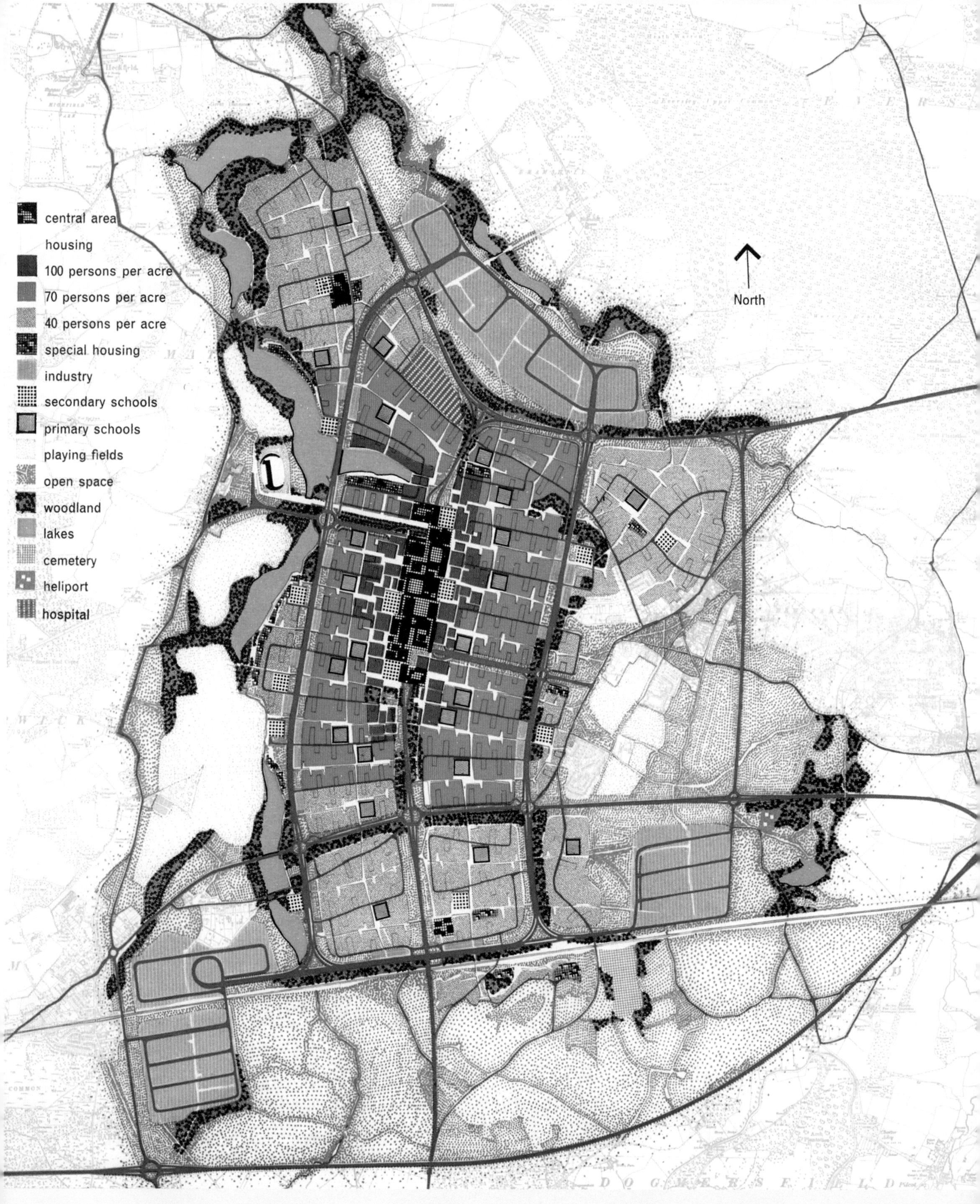
central area
housing
100 persons per acre
70 persons per acre
40 persons per acre
special housing
industry
secondary schools
primary schools
playing fields
open space
woodland
lakes
cemetery
heliport
hospital
North

HOOK

HAMPSHIRE, UK 1965

The great 'what if' of post-war British new towns. Plans for Hook New Town in Hampshire got remarkably far and were remarkably realized. What's striking about this project is the sheer quantity of visual material generated – the maps and plans almost like abstract paintings with lines and dots, though obviously scrupulously worked out by planners and engineers in smoky offices. The amount of drawings we still have from the project give the twenty-first-century urban archaeologist vivid views of what the finished city would have looked like. In many cases those visions were straight out of *Traffic in Towns* – a 1963 publication from the Ministry of Transport setting out plans to deal with projected future congestion problems – with a town centre raised above roads on a deck, complete segregation of cars and people throughout the new town, and a bold, muscular style of brutalist building that was surprising given how late this scheme came.

South-east London's sort-of-new-town Thamesmead was also being drawn up by the always progressive Greater London Council at this time and it too went crazy on concrete, decks and aggression, with a similar-ish house style to what was depicted for Hook. A recent visit to Thamesmead's Central (and earliest) section revealed extant raised decks and gloriously wilful architecture with a combative edge, but a sustained campaign of demolition occurring too to make it all more '2020s' (i.e. boring).

At the time, rival Milton Keynes – the last and largest of the new towns from the same era – embraced a very different low-rise, low-density approach without brutalism or decks, dismissing its own earlier, unrealized plans for a monorail and a more fantastical approach to cityscape. Transport and greenery were key elements of the design of Hook – minimal times for car travel around the city, easy motorway connections to the M3 and London and surrounding settlements like Basingstoke (chosen instead of Hook to become an expanded town), and plenty of green space. Hook was meant to be an 'overspill' city where Londoners would move, but also a fully functioning city with retail and industry. In the end Hook did evolve – in a less exciting way. Many new houses on suburban estates were built from the 1980s, but with none of the sci-fi excitement of the original plan.

OPPOSITE Map of the Hook New Town.

RIGHT Visions of a residential neighbourhood in Hook.

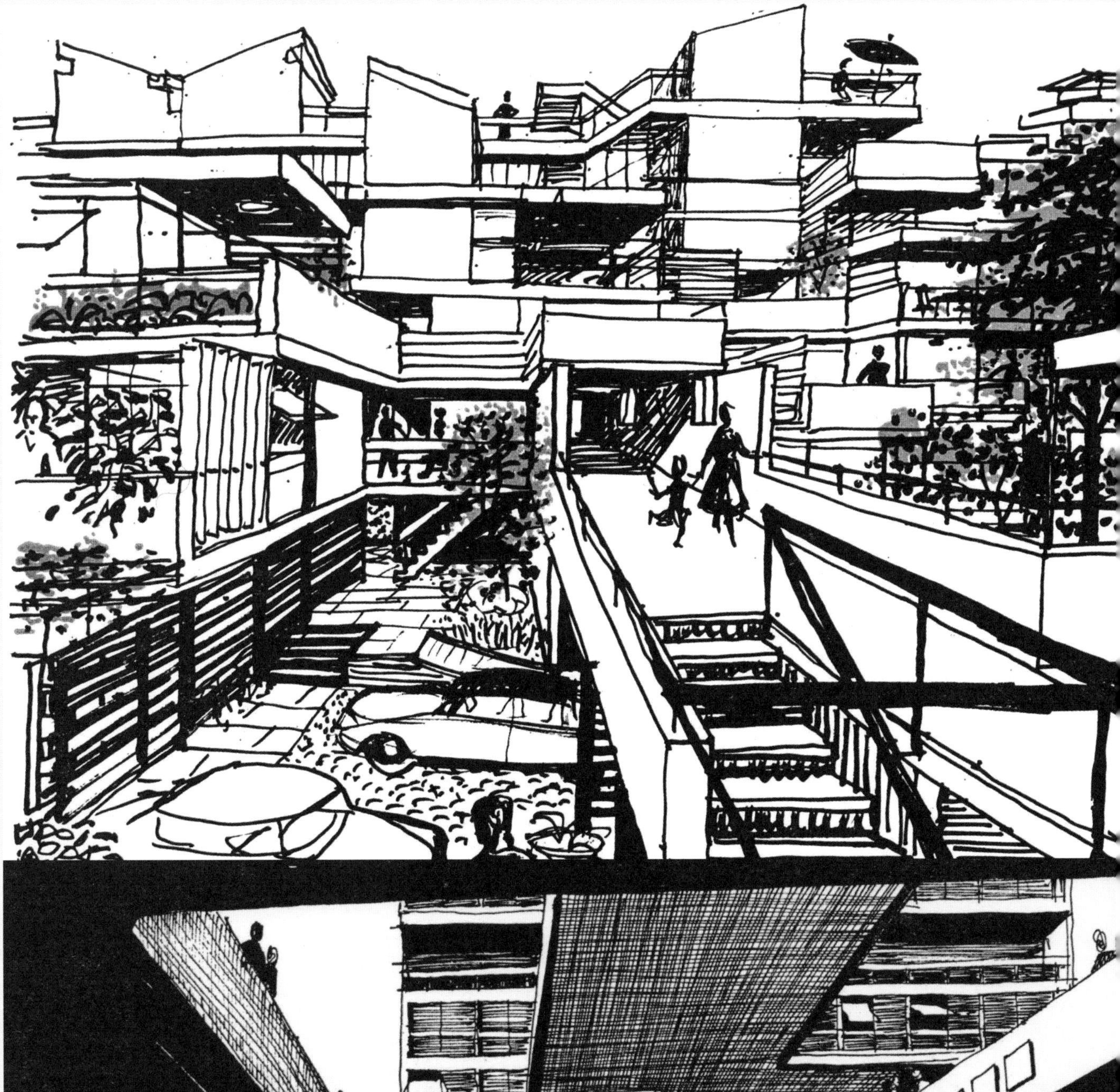

BAR
OXO
CAFE

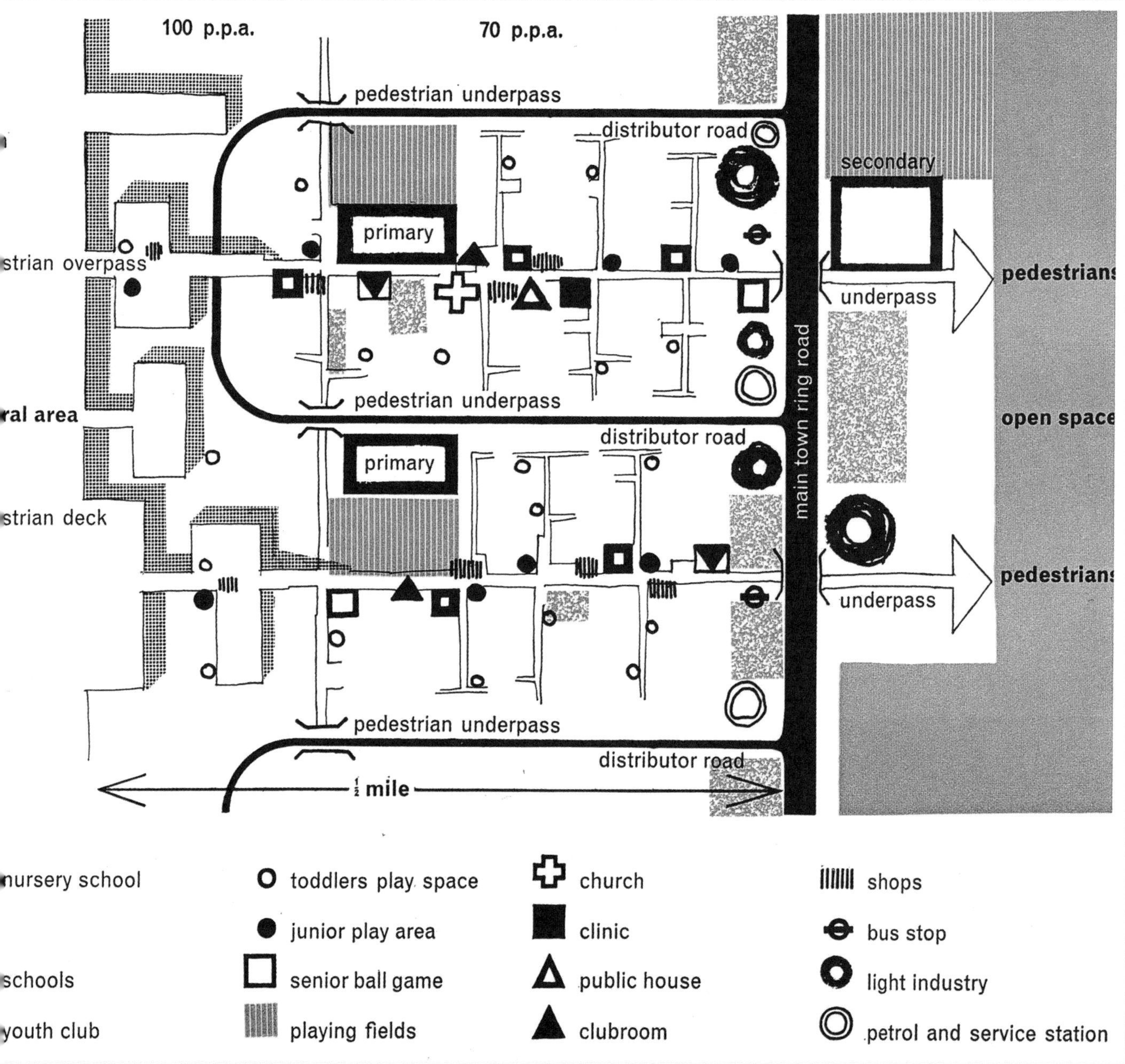

OPPOSITE, ABOVE A residential area.

OPPOSITE, BELOW Idea for how Hook town centre could look.

ABOVE Proposal for separation of functions in Hook New Town.

LA CITTA NUOVA

MILAN, ITALY 1914

Speed, technology, machines, science, movement. Antonio Sant'Elia's prophetic visualizations of the Italian or American city of the future were enough to get the cogs whirring in the brains of many modernists who kept faith with the idea that mass production, that cars, that velocity were the key drivers in modern architecture. The drawings look like they're from the pages of a comic – the spires and chimneys of the buildings ready for a superhero to pounce on.

Layers and levels were intrinsic to Sant'Elia's thoughts, likewise connections between buildings. Though none of this was ever constructed, the aesthetic went on to influence many over the following 50 years and the depictions seem as vibrant and intriguing today as they must have done over a century ago. One can even, perhaps, see echoes of the peculiarly busy aesthetic in Florence's weirdly postmodern-ish Palace of Justice by Leonardo Ricci from 2012.

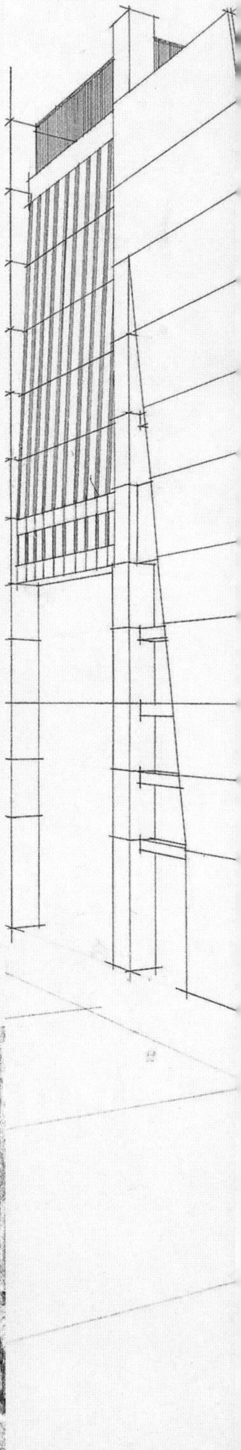

RIGHT La Citta Nuova, showing the many levels designed by Antonio Sant'Elia.

BELOW Project for the Station of Milan, 1914.

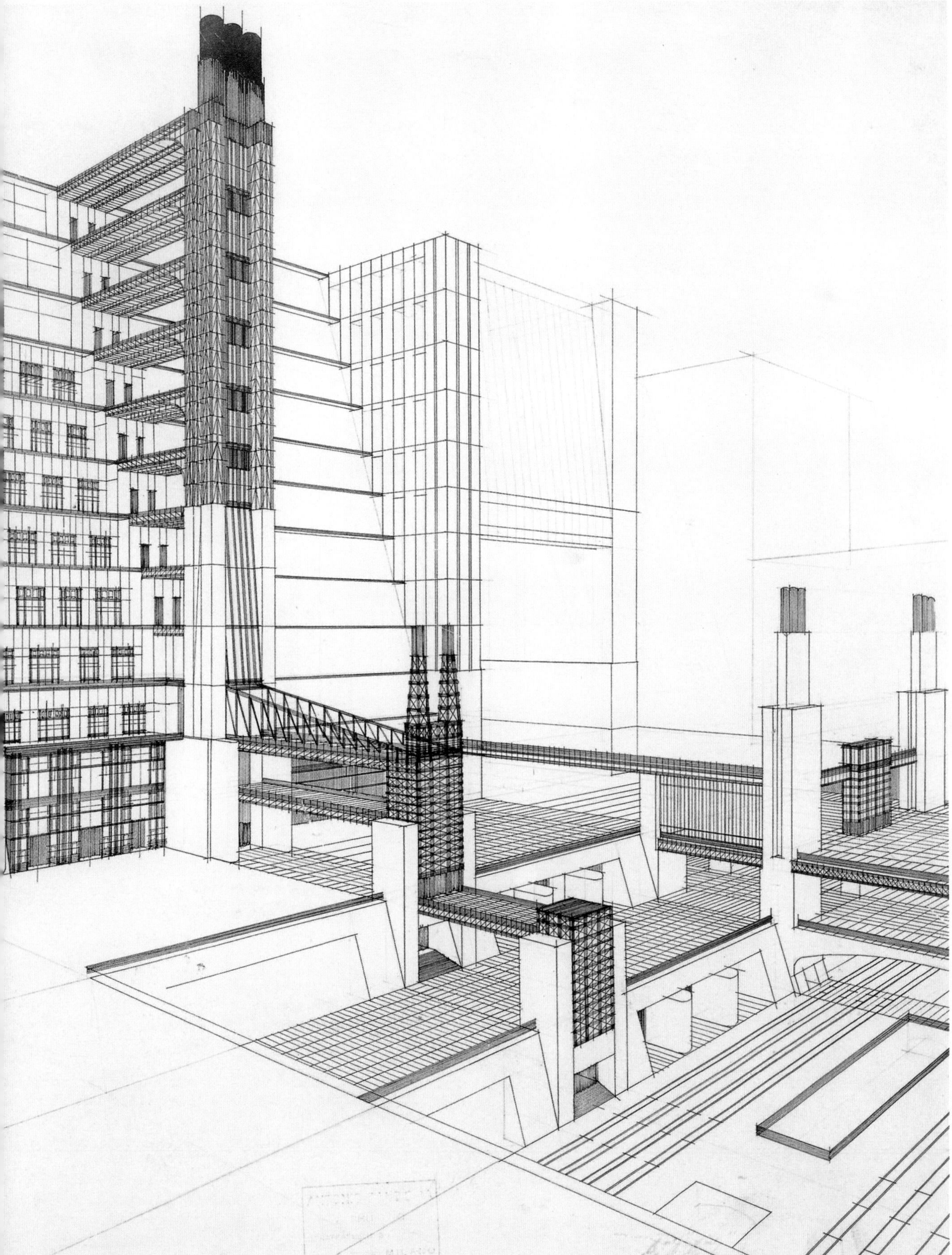

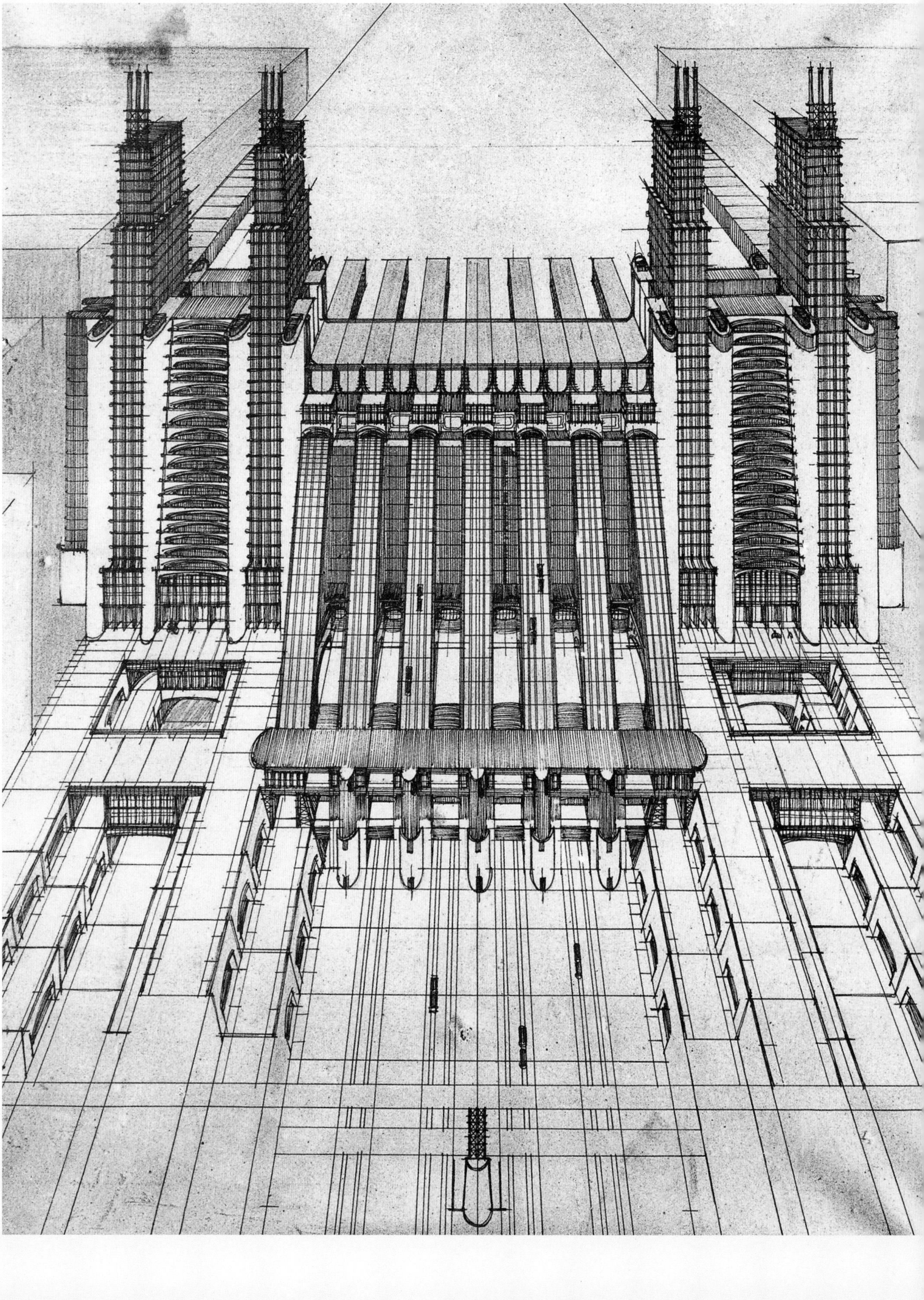

OPPOSITE AND LEFT Visions for the airport and train station of La Citta Nuova.

I'VE STARTED SO ... I'LL NEVER FINISH?

History is littered with examples of incomplete and unfinished architecture. Some of the world's most notorious exemplars have also become prime tourist traps: witness the crowds outside the Sagrada Familia, begun by Gaudí in 1882 on Barcelona's *modernisme* mile. There are hopes of it being finished in the 2030s. But who can really say? We want construction jobs finished in a year now because our lives have sped up (and developers want their money), but York Minster took 250 years to build, Ulm Cathedral and Cologne Cathedral took 600 and Stonehenge took 1,500.

Scotland's answer to Valhalla would have stood proud atop Calton Hill in Edinburgh – with graves of the great alongside those of the good who died in service to Scotland (and by then the UK) in military conflicts against France. Styled after the Parthenon, only a small fraction was built in the 1820s.

There's something about an abandoned shell of a building which is compelling in the extreme. The Britanika Hotel in Kaunas, Lithuania, still stands as a wreck. The hotel was to be a 500-room brutalist behemoth in 1989 but was never completed. During 2019's Kaunas Architecture Festival a rare opening occurred and 1,500 people partied on the windswept roof.

The Torre David in Caracas has become an unlikely icon of the struggles of the citizens, its new occupants trying to make the best of life above the chaos and hunger below. At its peak 5,000 squatted here in the shell of the skyscraper, no construction having taken place formally since 1994. Earthquakes caused considerable damage too.

Spain is riddled with motorways and *urbanizaciones* (suburbs) from the late 1990s and early 2000s that were built in a corrupt flurry and often never finished – their only real purpose being the backhanders the builders pocketed. A windswept car journey through the Levante's ghost towns is otherworldly: half-built houses, abandoned streets; from the air on a flight down to Alicante or Valencia or Almeria it all appears eerie.

Pyongyang's notorious empty and unfinished hotel the Ryugyong was begun in 1987 but has never opened and is far from finished. And even if it was, where would North Korea find the tourists to fill its rooms or the diners (or food, for that matter) for the five revolving restaurants atop this, the world's tallest unfinished building?

The more you look, the more you realize everything is a work in progress. The stubs of off-ramps, the streets that finish too soon, the walkways that were supposed to connect to something else, the doors to nowhere, the empty plots turned into hasty car parks. A full list would be endless: the Brunswick Centre was supposed to be longer, Thamesmead was supposed to have a Thames Bridge, Irvine was supposed to have a snaking megastructure and a more complete road layout, Liverpool's central area redevelopment was only a fraction of what was planned, Belfast's Divis Flats scheme was supposed to herald the start of a huge redevelopment of the entire Lower Falls Road, the fixed link mooted between the UK and Ireland is yet to arrive, and so it goes on ...

Nowhere is this 'unfinished' philosophy more evident than the airport: a structure in constant transition, like a celebrity who's never comfortable in their own flappy skin and is always restyling or getting injections and surgery. Every airport is always being amended: its size increased or reduced, retail swapped around, gates added, Schengen and non-Schengen zones split, new hotels, new roads, new stations, new access. Now it's new screens, walkways, one-way systems and social-distancing wheezes – the airport is almost like Archigram's Plug-in City, where things are moved around all the time and the architecture is impermanent. What's most hilarious is to look at how the modernist shells of once famous 'architectural' airports – like Foster's Stansted and Spence's Glasgow, and JFK, with its unique collection of once significant terminals by Pei and Saarinen – have all been defrocked, mocked and stocked with chain pubs and poke joints.

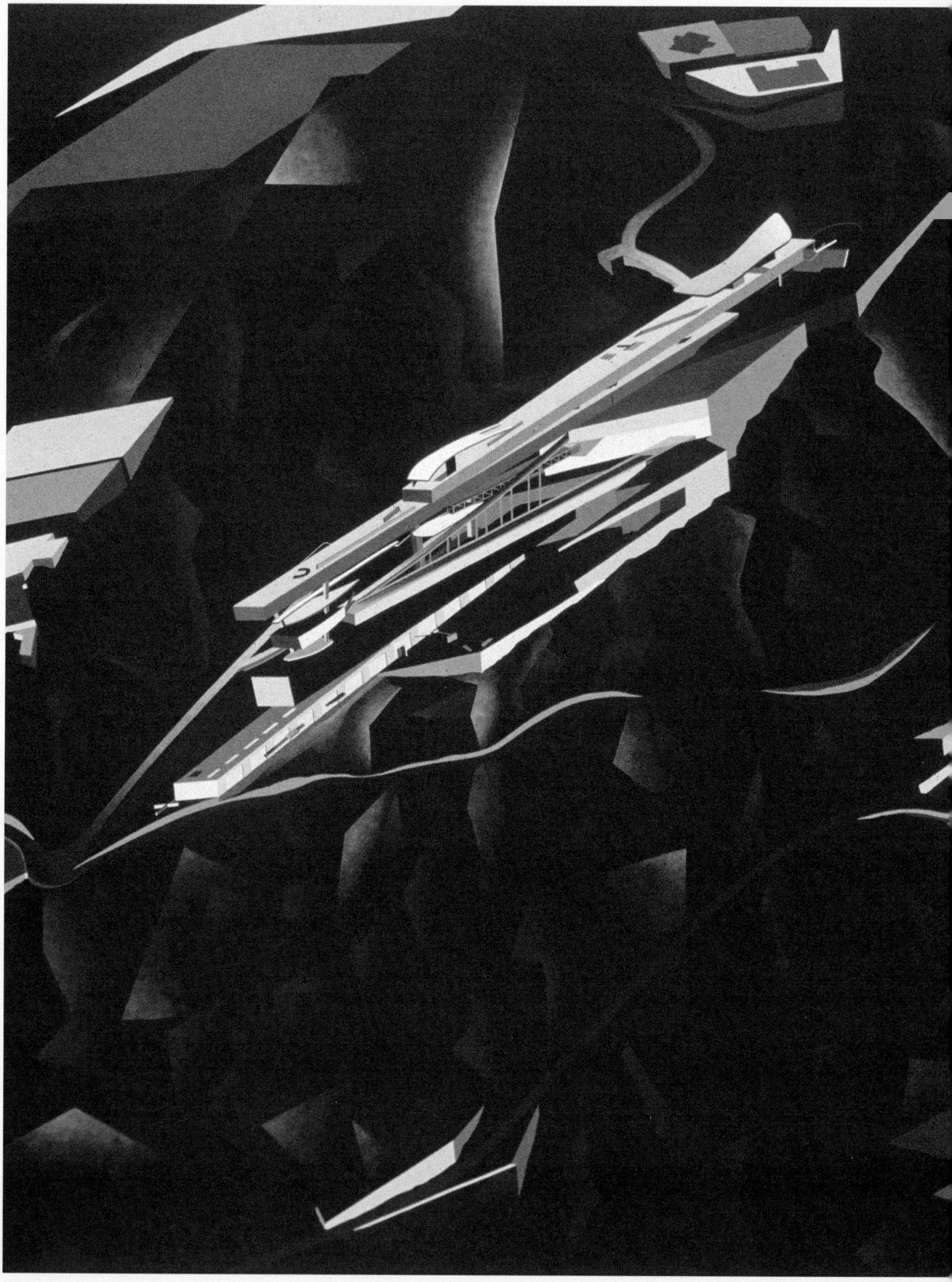

URBAN FANTASIES

'Megastructures cannot be described, they must be seen.'

PETER HALL

MANHATTAN DOME

NEW YORK, USA 1960

The dome is a delicious idea. Utterly barmy, of course, yet the appeal of it is not hard to see. The dome connotes safety, but it also plays with ideas of inclusion and exclusion. At the most primal level it harks back to our very atmosphere, the comfort blanket surrounding the Earth; the thing that would wipe us all out in a flash if it wasn't there tomorrow.

Artificially mimicking this notion of the atmosphere was a popular ruse in post-war America. It's no coincidence that it came at a time of deep paranoia, of Reds under the bed, of the Cuban Missile Crisis, of the greatest empire the world has ever known getting tetchy when it had no need to.

The dome's most famous exponent was Richard Buckminster Fuller – sci-fi dreamer, entrepreneur, wag, writer of odd sentences, conflicted builder of natural shapes on industrial scales. In 1960 he and Japanese architect Shoji Sadao conjured up a scheme to put a giant dome over midtown Manhattan.

The pros of the Domed City, they argued, were largely to do with climate control – a shrewd sales tactic in an air conditioning-obsessed nation. Mild winters, cool summers, no need for any buildings in the dome to run heating or cooling.

The bravado and insanity of the project captured the public mood in a country prone to both of those conditions. It was never built owing to the immense cost and the question of how to get in and out of the wretched thing. But Bucky was heartened; later, he planned a floating city – a spherical geodesic dome, heated, that would float above America. That never took off either.

Some domes did fly though: in 1958 Buckminster Fuller had, with Dick Lehr, built a works for the Union Tank Car Company in Baton Rouge, demolished 50 years after its construction. Railway wagons that carried oil from the city's refineries were maintained under the huge half-dome

PREVIOUS PAGE The Peak: Zaha Hadid's proposal for the highest mountain in Central Hong Kong, China.

LEFT Buckminster Fuller looks at dome models.

OPPOSITE Fuller's proposal for a dome over Manhattan.

that kept out the swamp sweat of the Louisiana summers. And for Expo 67 in Montreal, Bucky was tasked with designing the American offering – a giant geodesic dome with a podium and pavilion inside. The dome caught fire in 1976 and the image of the flaming structure, which seemed to augur the end of a richly optimistic, fantastical era of architectural posturing, was later purloined by Arcade Fire when the Montreal band were promoting their 2010 album *The Suburbs* online.

The dome recurred in pop culture – in *The Simpsons Movie* and the sci-fi TV series *Under the Dome*. But it never appeared over New York as Bucky really wished it had. One interesting postscript to consider: if it had been built, what of the rash of super-tall skyscrapers currently infecting Midtown, like 432 Park Avenue? Would they simply not have been built, or would holes have been drilled in the dome for them to puncture through towards the heavens, the oligarchs' apartments at the top of these terrible towers being, so very literally, beyond the pale?

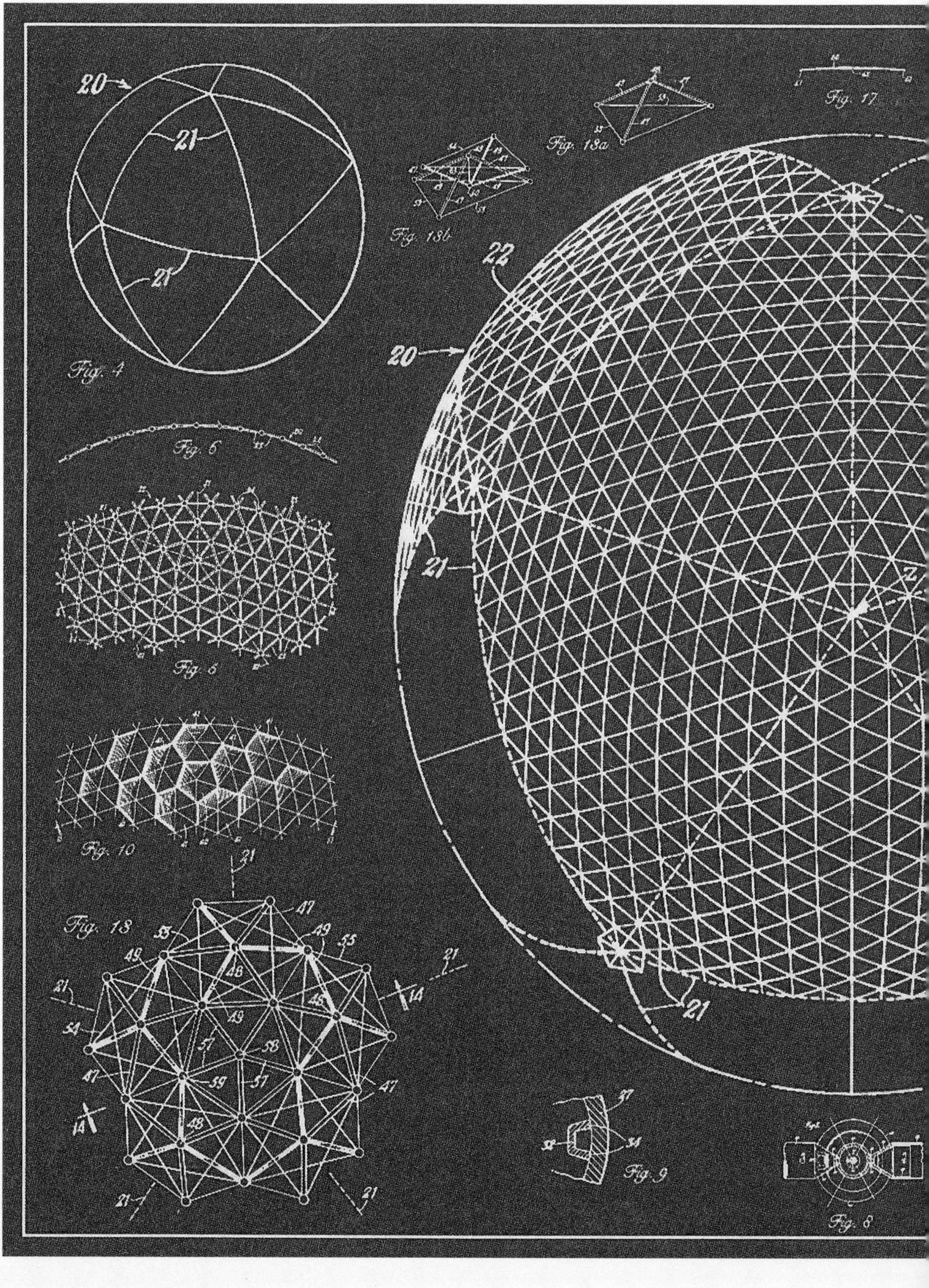
Fig. 4
Fig. 6
Fig. 5
Fig. 10
Fig. 18
Fig. 13b
Fig. 13a
Fig. 17
Fig. 9
Fig. 8
20
21
22

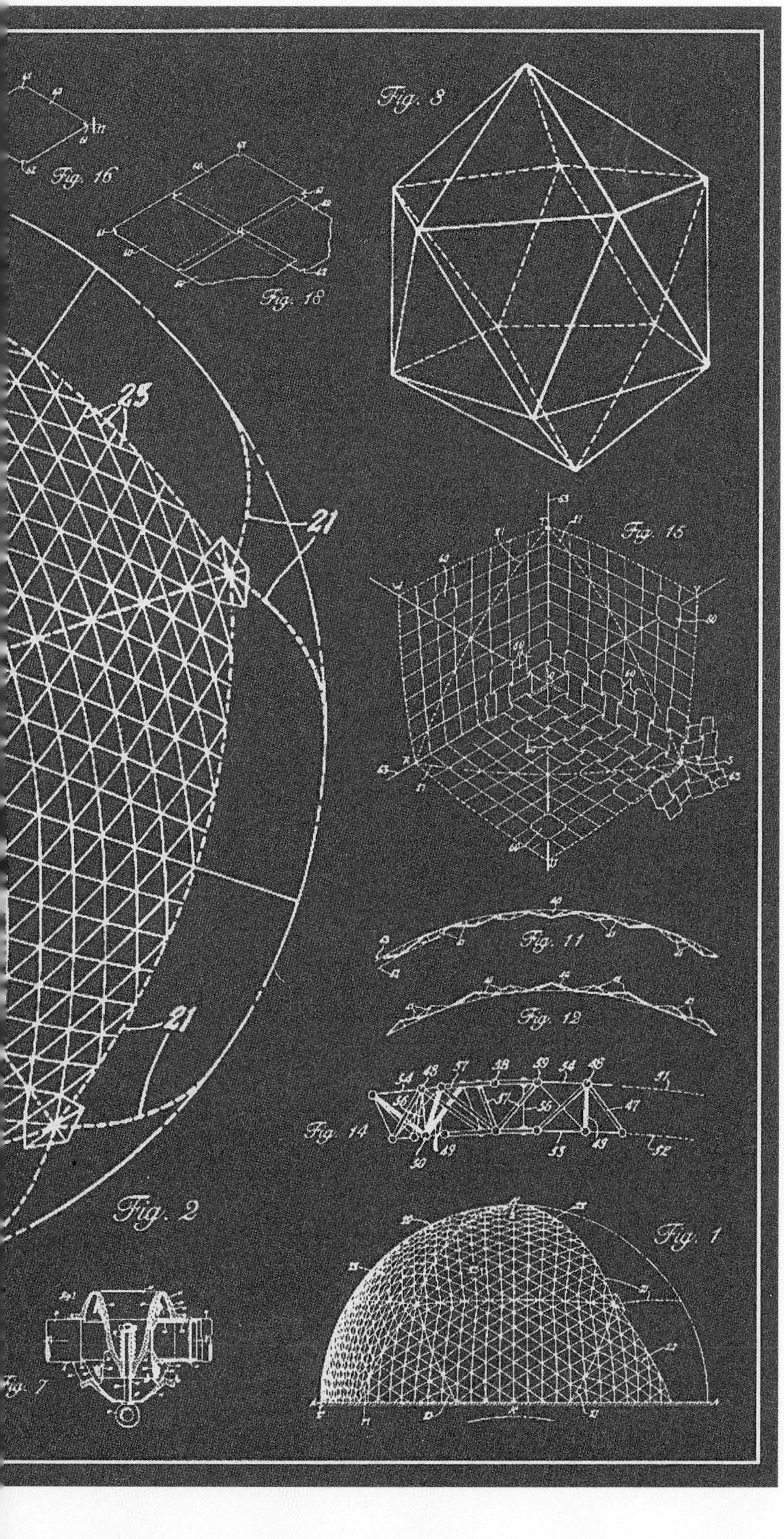

A blueprint for the Manhattan Dome.

THE SKOPJE THAT PARTIALLY WAS

SKOPJE, NORTH MACEDONIA 1960s

It looks like a press shot for a Krautrock band. The photo, which sadly we were unable to reproduce in this book, of Kenzō Tange's team in front of their model of the radical rebuilding of what is now the North Macedonian capital is something of a cult classic in modernist circles. The model shows in glorious 3D what Tange fans would have expected – an absolutely no-holds-barred slice of monumental metabolism with the city as a space station. People think the Skopje that was built under Tange and the later lead of Adolf Ciborowski was pretty radical, and it was, even though ultimately (in the scheme of things) just a few fragments went up like the showpiece station, post office and residential blocks.

They are all impressive – but this original plan would have created a totality – the world's most startling city carved from the ruins of the earthquake-ravaged city that was destroyed in 1963. Megastructures and highways would have stretched along great axes with flowing water at their centres, and with buildings ready to adapt over the years as per the metabolist philosophies of combining megastructures with organic biological growth, but the whole plan was never acted on, and watered down.

The postscript to this story is fascinating too – on a visit several years ago I observed the most banal statues being erected everywhere, and neo-classical façades being bolted on to the outside of those few brutalist wonders from the 1960s, the hare-brained schemes of nationalist politicians who have unwittingly created a Balkan Las Vegas when they could have had, if history had turned out differently, southern Europe's most serious city, a radical place that would have attracted urbanists and gawping Instagrammers from around the world.

LEFT Tange and his team examine a model for the ambitious rebuilding of Skopje that was only partially completed.

OPPOSITE, ABOVE AND BELOW Models exhibited in Zurich in 2013 as part of an exhibition looking back at the rebuilding of Skopje.

VILLE SPATIALE

TUNIS, MONACO, NEW YORK, PARIS, NICE 1958-1970s

The nearest analogy to the work of the French-Hungarian Yona Friedman is probably to imagine a cross between a bridge and a building (or even a bridge and a city). His series of Ville Spatiale proposals from 1958 onwards all involved moving life (and architecture) above ground, to leave the ground space empty, often cantilevering elements of the structure. The projects for Nice, Paris, New York were all intriguing.

At Monaco he wanted the Ville Spatiale to increase precious land by building over the Monte Carlo harbour; at Tunis, he wanted to build over the Medina. There was also a bridge-city plan to stretch across the English Channel rather like a super-length version of the first frenzied London Bridge, which teemed with buildings. Stacked capsules were a recurring design element; bigger volumes offered up in a slightly more palatable way were on the table too, like the unrealized plan – not quite as ambitious as Ville Spatiale – for a new Tanzanian Parliament in Dar es Salaam (1967).

LEFT A 1959 Ville Spatiale design.

OPPOSITE, ABOVE Perspective drawing of a Ville Spatiale design from 1960.

OPPOSITE, BELOW Photomontage of the Ville Spatiale across the harbour in Monaco.

CITY IN THE AIR

TOKYO, JAPAN 1962

Tree-like forms made the City in the Air stand out from other radical plans of the era. Arata Isozaki wanted to build tall concrete cores and then suspend architecture from them, leaving the ground plan of Tokyo relatively untouched while *homo ludens* would do their business up high. The onus was on the city being able to evolve – common to a lot of these theories – and the idea that bits could be plugged out or in.

Kenzō Tange's Shizuoka Press and Broadcasting Center has this core with offices cantilevered off it, but that didn't look like you could easily plug anything in or out when I looked at it. It gives an idea of the concept on a small scale but Isozaki wanted (no surprise, really) to go big, with the protruding branches much, much longer than Tange's try in the Ginza district of Tokyo. The effect of several of these structures placed together in the photomontage commonly used to explain the concept is striking.

OPPOSITE City in the Air, Shinjuku Project, 1960–61.

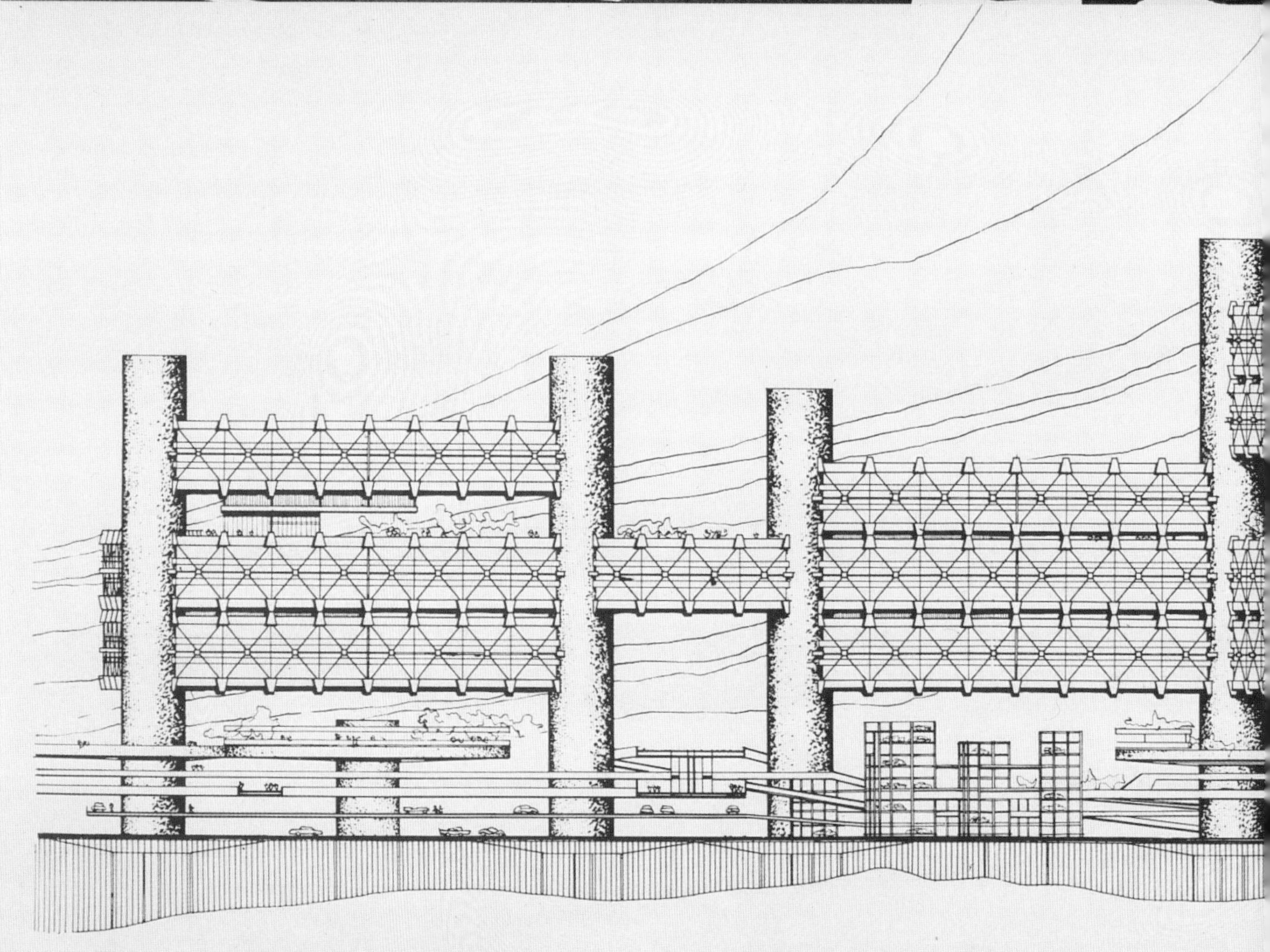

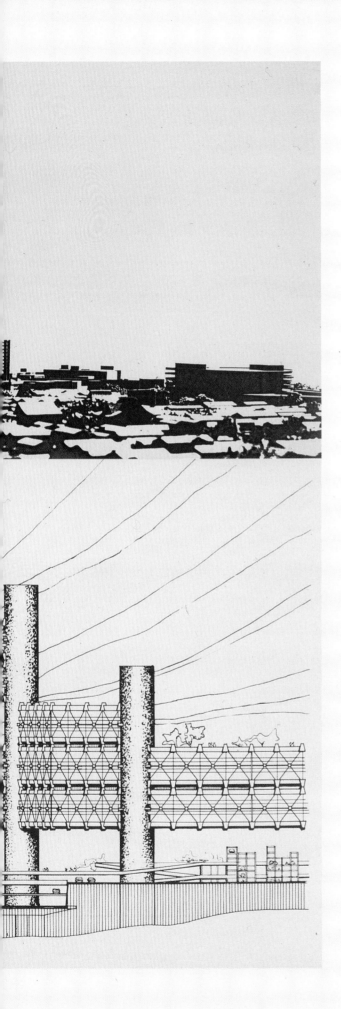

ABOVE LEFT City in the Air,
Shibuya Project, 1960–62.

LEFT City in the Air,
Shinjuku Project, 1960–61.

ZAHA HADID'S VISIONS

LONDON, HONG KONG, DUBLIN, MADRID, HAMBURG, TOKYO 1977-2016

'People do ask: "Why are there no straight lines, why no ninety degrees in your work?" This is because life is not made in a grid. If you think of a landscape, it's not even and regular – but people go to these places and think it's very natural.'

Zaha Hadid's words to me in a 2015 interview I conducted with her have stuck in my mind. Seeing her incredible early paintings and drawings that presaged some remarkable later built work, notably Rome's MAXXI Gallery, one is struck by a sense of ambition within the *surrealismo* of the scenes. Long before the curves came and the parametricism could be done by pushing a button on a computer keyboard, sharp lines and acute angles predominated in plans (not built) for actual buildings like the Irish Prime Minister's residence in Dublin (1979) and The Peak Leisure Club in Hong Kong (1983), and for the future development of Madrid, Hamburg and London.

Her works *Metropolis* and *The World* are intriguing as art in their own right and shone at the 1988 MoMA exhibition 'Deconstructivist Architecture' in New York, which also featured Frank Gehry and Daniel Libeskind.

One final postscript: Hadid won the competition to design the stadium for the 2020 Tokyo Olympics before her death, but organizers scrapped that plan and chose an alternative stadium. And then they had to postpone the whole Olympics due to the Covid-19 crisis, which unleashed a tsunami of chaos around the world in 2020. Best laid plans and all ...

Hadid's vision for The Peak, Hong Kong, China.

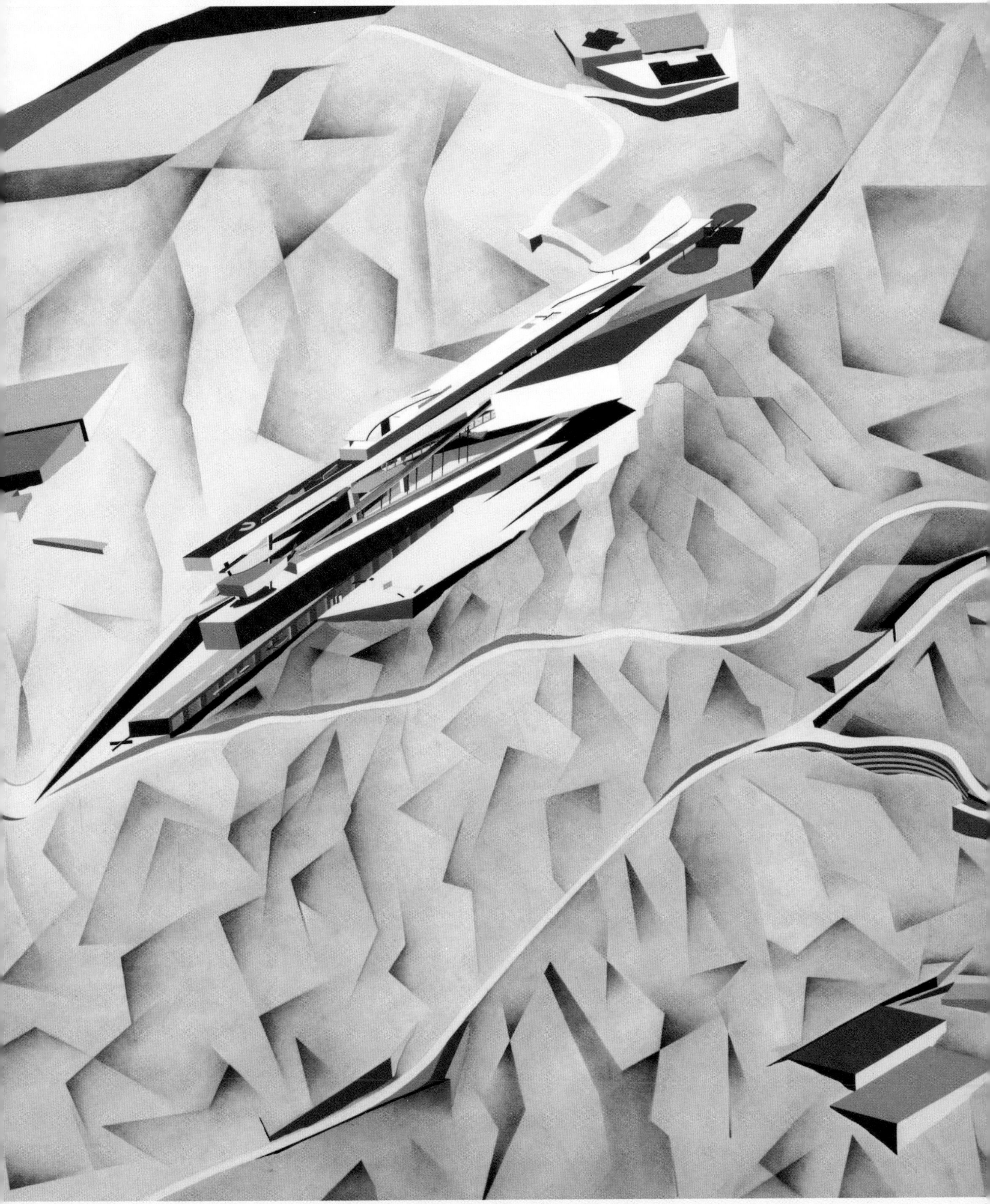

ABOVE Zaha Hadid pictured at her home in London.

LEFT Design for the Irish Prime Minister's residence in Dublin.

OPPOSITE The Peak, Hong Kong.

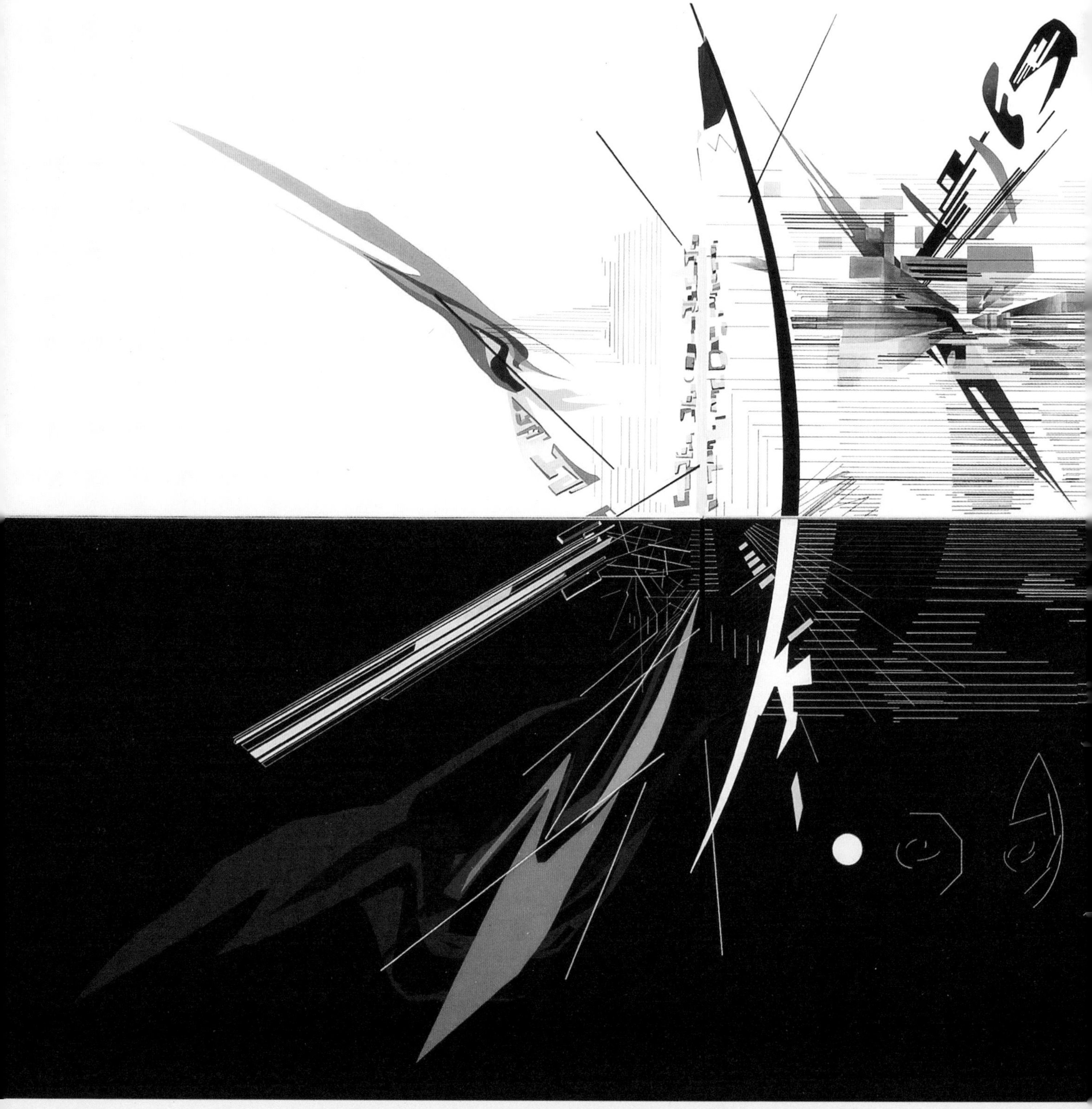

Zaha Hadid's Vision for Madrid. Hadid's paintings were unique in their surrealist imaginings of future cities.

The Peak, Hong Kong.

SUPER-TALL SKYSCRAPER CITIES

TOKYO, SAN FRANCISCO, HONG KONG, JEDDAH

1990s-PRESENT/FUTURE

More science fiction than science fact, the idea of building ever larger and ever higher vertical cities has caught the public attention – and indeed many of these plans seem as much designed for that purpose as actual engineering solutions for the future. Nevertheless, their absurd ambition makes them of interest. The X Seed 4000 was a 1995 idea from Peter Neville and the Taisei Corp to build a 4km (2½ mile) high city shaped like Mount Fuji, which would rest on the sea bed and house one million souls. How you would clean the windows wasn't mentioned.

The Shimizu Mega City Pyramid was a pyramid-shaped superstructure idea from the Shimizu Corporation in 2004 that would be 2km (1¼ miles) high and again house that magic million people. Eugene Tsui's 1991 Ultima Tower was intended to be 1,800m (6,000ft) tall and could have been built by the sea at Hong Kong or San Francisco.

Tall buildings continue to be popular though – with the sought-after title of 'the tallest in the world' propelling engineers and architects to push the boundaries of what's possible. The tallest building in the world will be the Jeddah Tower, at over 1km (⅔ mile) high, when that is finished. But the tower could merit its own mention here, as it was incomplete with construction stalled when this book was first published in 2021 – despite work having begun back in 2013. When it will finally complete is currently anyone's guess.

HELIX CITY

TOKYO, JAPAN 1961

Kisho Kurokawa worked alongside those other titans of post-war Japanese futurism who gave that country such a push towards the new technological world – Fumihiko Maki and Arata Isozaki, and Kenzō Tange. Kurokawa's big idea was the Helix (or, as Banham called it, Helicoidal) City. Inspired no doubt by the recent mapping of the structure of DNA in the 1950s by James Watson and Francis Crick, Kurokawa's supersized helixes aped that natural pattern as an intended intersection between the organic and inorganic worlds. His twisted skyscrapers would interconnect into one long line, and sit over both water and land. Kurokawa went on to build one of the emblems of metabolism – the stacked-up washing machines of the Nakagin Capsule Tower in Tokyo – which is grimly still hanging on to its existence, or at least was the last time I went to marvel at its Tetris textures and, unsurprisingly, bumped into an architecture student there who was doing the same.

Kurokawa's Helix City vision.

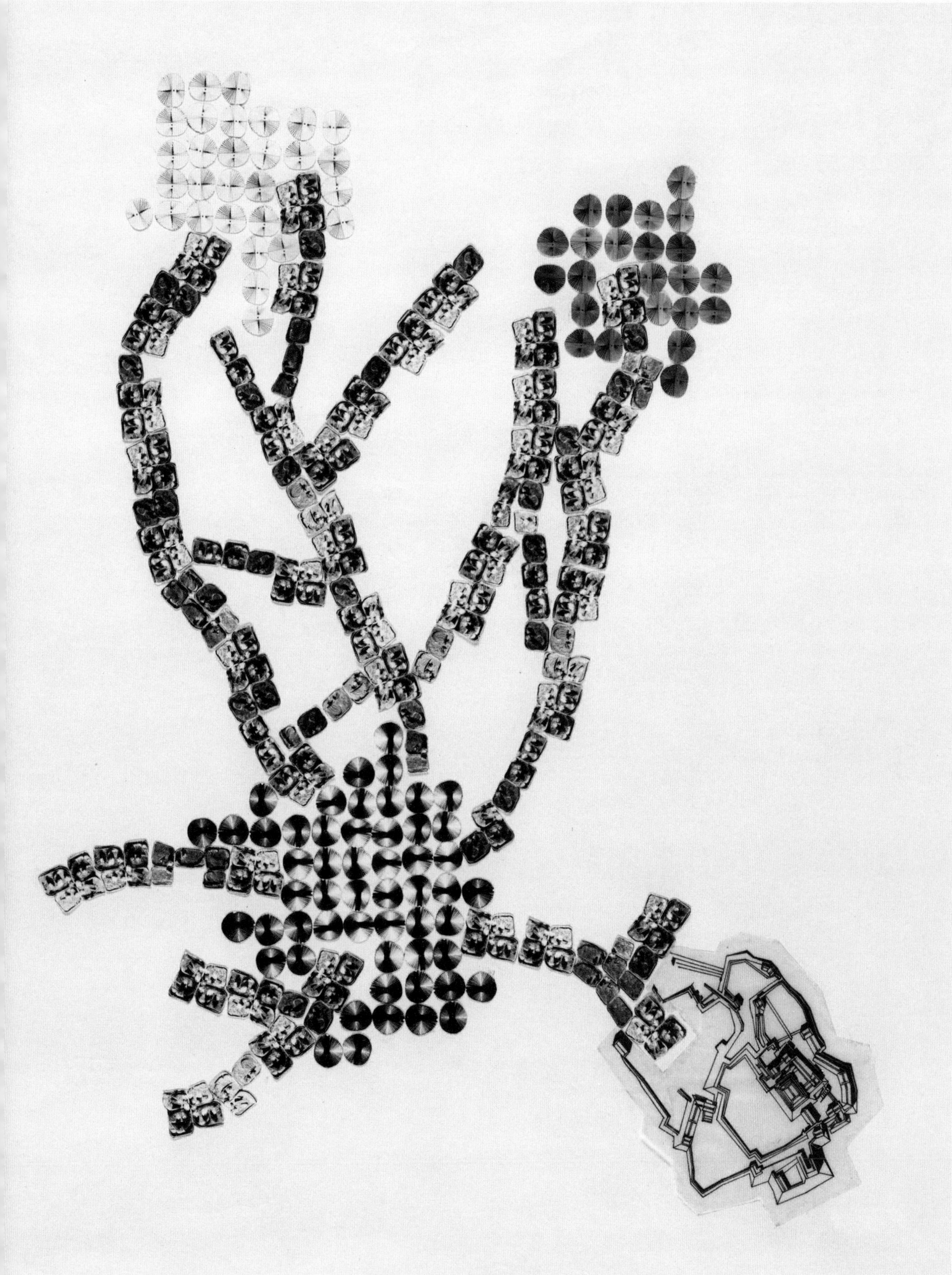

ARCHIGRAM'S PROJECTS

WORLDWIDE 1960s

Ron Herron's Walking City has a touch of Terry Gilliam's *Monty Python* cartoons about its look, and a *Black Mirror*-esque aftertaste in its prediction of a post-apocalyptic world. The constantly moving robotic pods on legs would traverse a potentially shattered future, keeping safe their inhabitants inside. Peter Cook, Herron's co-conspirator in the 1960s avant-garde architectural group Archigram, took the lead on the trendy Plug-in City idea, beautifully realized in attractive Meccano-like depictions which promulgated the idea's spread in magazines and radical journals. The primary colours and spacey sensibilities of the project to build high-tech megastructures, but ones in which parts could be craned into and out of the frame, spoke with a kind of Swinging Sixties lexicon one supposes. They came from a London that was in the cultural ascendancy and where modern architecture was exploding (unlike sleepy, post-Brexit, post-pandemic London in 2021).

Archigram's visual language, experimentation and – ultimately – the unbuildability of their projects gave them a certain piquancy and almost advocated for the idea of not building, of just dreaming up radically provocative ideas instead. That said, Jonathan Meades elucidates in a *London Review of Books* appraisal of *Archigram: The Book* that 'its insouciant epigoni made their designs real', and that its members turned up to the Pompidou 'gobsmacked' that their ideas had been apparently purloined. 'Being too original scares the punters,' he says. 'Founders never prosper.'

Their plans for Monaco used collage to elaborate on a certain sleazy glitz.

LEFT Walking City, as envisaged by Archigram.

OPPOSITE, ABOVE Plan for the Plug-in City.

OPPOSITE, BELOW Vision of Monte Carlo, glamly imagined by Archigram.

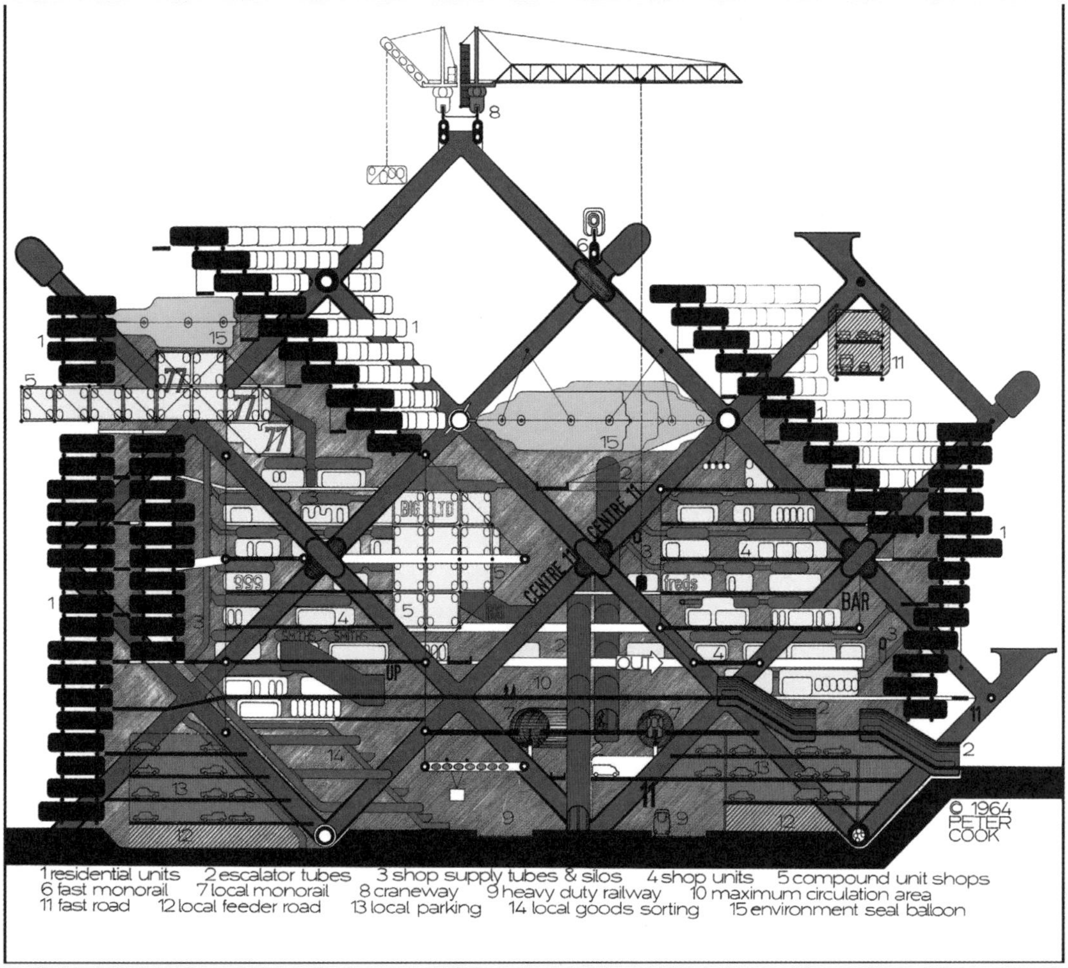
BIG LTD
CENTRE 11
freds
BAR
UP
OUT
© 1964 PETER COOK
1 residential units 2 escalator tubes 3 shop supply tubes & silos 4 shop units 5 compound unit shops
6 fast monorail 7 local monorail 8 craneway 9 heavy duty railway 10 maximum circulation area
11 fast road 12 local feeder road 13 local parking 14 local goods sorting 15 environment seal balloon

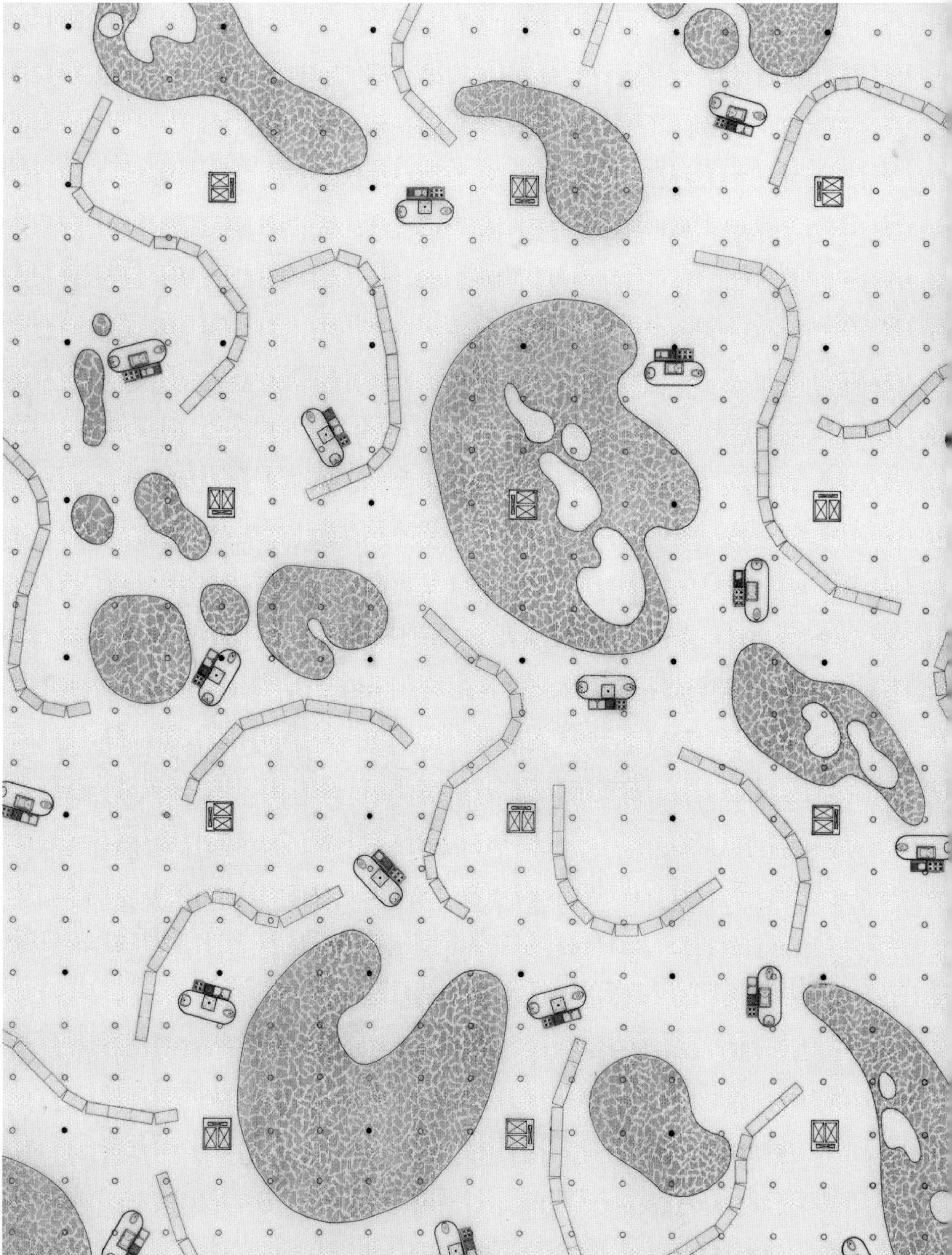

NO-STOP CITY AND CONTINUOUS MONUMENT

FLORENCE, ITALY 1969

The 1960s saw two radical city plans emerge from Tuscany, which pushed the boundaries at the end of a decade of incredible ambition and creativity. Archizoom's No-Stop City is a bleak, bare, endless and empty megastructure, which can be filled with furniture and stretches forever like a scaled-up computer circuit board; one wonders if the makers of *Tron* had it in their thoughts? Superstudio's Continuous Monument appears in the visualizations as a kind of parasitic architecture, the Harvey Weinstein of megastructures; an unsavoury white block with legs and an insectoid nature that has fondled the entire Earth, marching over natural forms and wrapping around existing cities like New York as if Le Corbusier's Plan Obus has caught coronavirus.

Both groups had gone to Florence University but both imagined one architecture running riot around the whole world. 'Where Archizoom demonstrated "cities without architecture" Superstudio's proposals were "architecture without cities",' says Douglas Murphy in his book *Last Futures*.

OPPOSITE Residential Park, No-Stop City, project plan, 1969.

ABOUT THE AUTHOR

Christopher Beanland is the author of the non fiction books *Lido* and *Concrete Concept: Brutalist Buildings Around The World* and the novels *The Wall In The Head* and *Spinning Out of Control*. He is also the writer of many pieces of journalism. He lives in London.
Instagram @christopherbeanland
Twitter @chrisbeanland

THANKS

Thanks to: Joss Durnan, Tina Richardson, Elain Harwood, londonist.com, Will Dean for commissioning the original London Ringways story and all at *The Independent*, all at Berlinische Galerie, Eliana Pavel, Rebecca Lane, Steve Pill, Nigel Cottier, James Ward for the author photo, Damjan Kokalevski, Andre McLeod, Jason Sayer, Laura Mintz, Roisin Inglesby, Stuart and everyone at Glasgow Motorway Archive, Irene and all at Glasgow City Archives, Larry Blow, the International Maglev Board and everyone in the Maglev community, who have always been so welcoming, and Nick Mead at *The Guardian* for commissioning me to write about Maglev for them. Beatrice Cooke and all at RIBA, Mae-Li Evans and all at *Monocle*, Nick Francis, who is working with me on a podcast series linked to the ideas in here.

Everyone at Batsford including Tina Persaud and Lucy Smith for commissioning and always believing in my ideas, Frida Green, Lilly Phelan, Jennifer Veall, Gemma Doyle, Sally Bond and, most importantly, my brilliant editor Nicola Newman. Everyone else who helped source photos and images for the book.

Nicky Trup for endless inspiration.

My mum, dad and brother for always being the best supporters.

This book evolved out of a series of articles I wrote for NESTA's magazine *The Long And Short* from 2015 onwards. Special thanks to Larry Ryan, and the team there, for starting this ball rolling.

PICTURE CREDITS

2 Pictures From History/CPA Media Pte Ltd/Alamy Stock Photo; 4–5, 45, 46–47, 48, 49 Schenkung Elisabeth von Sartory und Georg Kohlmaier, 2015. Repro: Anja Elisabeth Witte/Berlin Museum of Modern Art. © DACS 2021; 12 Courtesy of the National Archives of Australia, NAA: A710, 7; 14–15 Bill Ellman/Mirrorpix; 16–17 Nick Maslen/ Alamy Stock Photo; 18 Reproduced with the permission of the Library of Birmingham; 19 Architectural Press Archive / RIBA Collections; 21 © Glasgow City Archives; 22 IanDagnall Computing / Alamy Stock Photo; 22–23 The Frank Lloyd Wright Fdn, AZ / Art Resource, NY/Scala, Florence. © ARS, NY and DACS, London 2021; 24 Photograph © 2021 Carnegie Museum of Art, Pittsburgh. © ARS, NY and DACS, London 2021; 26–27 National Library of Australia; 28–29 National Archives of Australia: NAA: A710, 31; 29 (top) National Archives of Australia: NAA: A710, 34; 29 (bottom) National Archives of Australia: NAA: A710, 23; 30 (top) National Archives of Australia: NAA: A710, 1; 30 (bottom) National Archives of Australia: NAA: A710, 4; 31 (top) National Archives of Australia: NAA: A710, 13; 31 (bottom) National Archives of Australia: NAA: A710, 10; 32 (top), 32–33 (top), 32–33 (bottom), 33 (bottom) © The Architectural Review, October 1975; 34–35 INTERFOTO/Alamy Stock Photo; 36–37, 40 (bottom); 37, 38, 40 (top) INTERFOTO/Alamy Stock Photo; 39 REUTERS/Johannes Eisele/Alamy Stock Photo; 41 Pictures From History/CPA Media Pte Ltd/Alamy Stock Photo; 42, 56 Album/Alamy Stock Photo; 50–51 Roger-Viollet/Shutterstock. © F.L.C./ADAGP, Paris and DACS, London 2021; 52–53, 53 (top), 54–55, 98–99, 100, 101 (bottom) Le Corbusier Foundation. © F.L.C./ADAGP, Paris and DACS, London 2021; 57 Ivan Vdovin / Alamy Stock Photo; 58, 59 SPUTNIK / Alamy Stock Photo 60–61, 144 (top) Heritage Image Partnership Ltd / Alamy Stock Photo; 64–65 Photo by Hans Werlemann, courtesy OMA; 66, 67, 68–69 Courtesy OMA; 70–71, 72, 73 (top) Louis I Kahn Collection, The University of Pennsylvania and the Pennsylvania Historical and Museum Collection; 73 (bottom), 195 © 2021. Digital image, The Museum of Modern Art, New York/ Scala, Florence; 74, 76, 76–77 David Rumsey Map Collection, David Rumsey Map Center, Stanford Libraries; 75 State of California, Department of Public Works/Wikipedia; 80, 92–93 (top), 92–93 (bottom) Cedric Price fonds / Canadian Centre for Architecture; 82–83, 84 (top), 84 (bottom) © The Lunuganga Trust; 86 Bauhaus-Archiv Berlin. © DACS; 87 akg-images. © DACS; 89 (top), 89 (bottom), 90 Fairfax Photographic Archive/Sydney Morning Herald/Stuart McGladrie; 91 Fairfax Photographic Archive/Sydney Morning Herald; 94, 120–121, 122, 123, 124, 125, 126 (top), 126 (bottom); 127 Library of Congress; 96–97, 110–111 Keystone Press/Alamy Stock Photo; 101 (top) Digital image, The Museum of Modern Art, New York/Scala, Florence. © F.L.C./ADAGP, Paris and DACS, London 2021; 102–103 © Clifford Stead; 104 Mtaylor848, licensed under the Creative Commons Attribution-ShareAlike 3.0 Unported licence (https://creativecommons.org/licenses/by-sa/3.0/legalcode); 105, 106–107 Leeds Library & Information Services; 108 Robert Evans / Alamy Stock Photo; 112 (top left) © National Archives; 112 (top right) © London Metropolitan Archives, City of London GLC/DG/ PUB/01/0380; 112 (bottom) © London Metropolitan Archives, City of London GLC/TD/DP/LDS/01/097; 113 (top) The Underground Map, licensed under the Creative Commons Attribution-Share Alike 2.0 Generic licence (https://creativecommons.org/licenses/by-sa/2.0/legalcode); 114 UrbanImages / Alamy Stock Photo; 116–117 Ulrich Doering/ Alamy Stock Photo; 119 NASA/Alamy Stock Photo; 120 Bettmann/Getty Images; 130, 146–147 © Foster + Partners; 133 Fox Photos/Getty Images; 134–135, 142–143 ullstein bild via Getty Images; 136, 137 © Historic England Archive; 138–139 ZUMA Press, Inc. / Alamy Stock Photo; 140 EuroStyle Graphics / Alamy Stock Photo; 141 (top) Yvan Leduc under the Creative Commons Attribution-Share Alike 3.0 Unported licence (https://creativecommons.org/licenses/by-sa/3.0/legalcode); 141 (bottom) Dtmf1313 under the Creative Commons Attribution-Share Alike 4.0 International licence (https://creativecommons.org/licenses/by-sa/4.0/legalcode); 144 (bottom left) Mirrorpix; 144 (bottom right) © National Railway Museum / Science & Society Picture Library -- All rights reserved; 148 (top) Frans Blok / Alamy Stock Photo; 148 (bottom) Dobbins Collection, Pasadena Museum of History; 149 Matthew James Harrison / Alamy Stock Photo; 150, 152–153, 154, 155 (left), 155 (right), 156 © Estates of Kenneth Browne and Hubert de Cronin Hastings, by permission of Artifice Press; 158 Album/akg-images. © ARS, NY and DACS, London 2021; 158–159 Granger Historical Picture Archive / Alamy Stock Photo. © ARS, NY and DACS, London 2021; 161 (top) CBS via Getty Images; 161 (bottom) Northwest Architectural Archives; 162, 163, 164 (top), 164 (bottom), 165 © London Metropolitan Archives, City of London GLC/DG/PUB/091/020; 166, 167, 168, 169 DEA PICTURE LIBRARY/De Agostini via Getty Images; 172, 186–187, 188 (bottom), 189, 190–191, 192 © Zaha Hadid Foundation; 174 © Tallandier / Bridgeman Images; 175 Courtesy the Estate of R. Buckminster Fuller; 176–177 Science Source/akg-images; 178, 179 (top), 179 (bottom) © Damjan Kokalevski; 180, 181 (top), 181 (bottom) Courtesy of the Fonds de Dotation Denise and Yona Friedman. © ADAGP, Paris and DACS, London; 183, 184–185 (top), 184–185 (bottom) © Arata Isozaki, courtesy of Arata Isozaki & Associates; 188 (top) Steve Speller / Alamy Stock Photo; 196 © Ron Herron Archive. All Rights Reserved, DACS/Artimage 2021; 197 (top)© Archigram 1964; 197 (bottom); © Archigram Architects 1972; 198 Digital image, The Museum of Modern Art, New York/Scala, Florence. © ADAGP, Paris and DACS, London 2021; 200 © James Ward.

London Ringways originally appeared as an article in *The Independent*. © The Independent 2011. Maglev, The Bruce Plan for Glasgow, King's Cross Airport, Pittsburgh Civic Centre, Tokyo Bay Plan, Manhattan Dome, Motopia, and Berlin's Post War Rebuilding all originally appeared in NESTA's *The Long And Short* in 2015 and 2016 (thelongandshort.org) and are republished here under a Creative Commons licence.

All reasonable efforts have been taken to ensure that the reproduction of the content in this book is done with the full consent of the copyright owners. If you are aware of unintentional omissions, please contact the company directly so that any necessary corrections may be made for future editions.

BIBLIOGRAPHY

Books and magazines

The Architectural Review, 15 October 1975: article on the Smithsons' Brasilia plan

Banham, Reyner: *Megastructure: Urban Futures of the Recent Past* (Monacelli Press, 2020)

Clawley, Alan: *John Madin* (Historic England, 2011)

Clawley, Alan: *Library Story: A History of Birmingham Central Library* (2016)

Crinson, Mark: *Alison and Peter Smithson* (Historic England, 2018)

Crompton, Dennis, Warren Chalk, Peter Cook, Ron Herron, David Greene, Michael Webb: *Archigram: the Book* (Princeton Architectural Press, 1999)

de Wolfe, Ivor (Hubert de Cronin Hastings): *Civilia: The End of Sub Urban Man* (The Architectural Press, 1971)

Goldin, Greg and Sam Lubell: *Never Built Los Angeles* (Metropolis Books, 2013)

Goldin, Greg and Sam Lubell: *Never Built New York* (Metropolis Books, 2016)

Grindrod, John: *Concretopia: The Rebuilding of Postwar Britain* (Old Street Publishing, 2014)

Harwood, Elain: *Chamberlin, Powell and Bon* (RIBA, 2011)

Murphy, Douglas: *Last Futures: Nature, Technology and the End of Architecture* (Verso Books, 2015)

O'Flynn, Catherine: *The News Where You Are* (Penguin, 2010)

The City of London Plan (1971)

Websites

The Civilia Project, Newcastle University (civilia.photo.blog)

londonist.com

ianvisits.co.uk

99 Percent Invisible (99percentinvisible.org)

glasgowmotorwayarchive.org

Films and TV

Dreaming the Impossible: Unbuilt Britain (BBC, 2013)

The Experimental City, directed by Chad Freidrichs (mxcfilm.com, 2017)

Glasgow 1980 (1971)

Paradise Lost: The Birmingham Central Library Story, directed by Andy Howlett (2021)

The Shock Of The New: 'Trouble in Utopia' episode (BBC, 2012)

I am grateful to Joel Newman and the Audiovisual Department at the Architectural Association for uploading video of talks by Reyner Banham on Megastructures (1974) and Alison and Peter Smithson on their projects (1976). Both were fascinating.

INDEX

Illustration references are in *italics*.

First published in the United Kingdom in 2021 by
Batsford
43 Great Ormond Street
London
WC1N 3HZ

ISBN 978-1-84994-663-6

A CIP catalogue record for this book is available from the British Library.

10 9 8 7 6 5 4 3 2 1

Reproduction by Rival Colour Ltd, UK
Printed and bound by 1010 Printing International Ltd, China

FSC
www.fsc.org
MIX
Paper from responsible sources
FSC® C016973